The Art of French Glass
1860-1914

JANINE BLOCH-DERMANT graduated from the École du Louvre following four years of specialized study in 19th-century art. Immediately thereafter she was admitted to a select group formed under the aegis of the Musée National de Sèvres to study *les arts du feu* ("the arts of fire" — glass and ceramic.) First published in 1974, her book became an instant success on the Continent, and the original French edition has now been reprinted several times. It serves as an official reference book at France's Centre National de la Recherche Scientifique (CNRS) and at the École du Louvre. In pursuit of her art historical interests, Mme Bloch-Dermant has traveled extensively in Russia, Great Britain, and Italy.

The Art of French Glass

1860-1914

Janine Bloch-Dermant

The Vendome Press

NEW YORK · PARIS · LAUSANNE

Translated by Marian Burleigh-Motley
Edited by Daniel Wheeler
Design concept by Max Thommen

Acknowledgments   The author wishes to express her warmest
thanks to all who helped in the preparation of this book, most
especially M. Raymond Chambon, curator at the Musée
du Verre at Charleroi, for his advice and encouragement, and
M. Jean-Claude Brugnot, Paris, for his full and active cooperation.
A particular debt of gratitude is owed to the curators of the
following museums: Musée des Arts Décoratifs, Paris;
Musée d'Art Moderne, Paris; Conservatoire des Arts et Métiers, Paris;
Musée Galliéra, Paris; Musée National de Céramique, Sèvres;
Musée du Petit-Palais, Paris. Of inestimable value was the
assistance received from Mlle T.M. Charpentier, curator of the
Musée de l'École de Nancy in Nancy. Collectors were also
generous, most of all M. Barlach Heuer, Paris;
Mme Maria de Beyrie, Paris; M. Pierre Boiteux, Paris;
M. Stéphane Deschamps, Paris; M. Günther Knut, Frankfurt;
Professor Helmut Hentrich, Düsseldorf; M. and Mme Alain Lesieutre, Paris;
M. Jacques Lorch, Paris; M. Félix Marcilhac, Paris;
M. Manoukian, Paris; M. and Mme Michel Périnet, Paris;
M. Jean-Pierre Strauss, Paris; Mlle Lyne Thornton;
M. and Mme Robert Walker, Paris; MM. Weymans and Meurrens, Brussels;
in addition to M. Michel Daum, Nancy; M. Jean-Pierre Comard;
Mme Jean Prouvé; Mme François Décorchemont; M. François Duret-Robert.
Finally, the author acknowledges with deep appreciation
the friendly assistance provided by Mme Gilberte Courtois.

Distributed by The Viking Press
625 Madison Avenue, New York, N.Y. 10022

Published simultaneously in Canada by Penguin Books Canada Limited

This edition published in 1980 in Great Britain by
Thames and Hudson, 30–34 Bloomsbury Street, London WC1B   3QP

Library of Congress Catalog Card Number: 80–50853

ISBN: 0–86565–000–4
Printed in Hong Kong
by South China Printing Co.

Contents

INTRODUCTION

Art begins the moment that man goes beyond the utilitarian designs of animals, and seeks instead to represent *or to* express *something. And whether representing or expressing, he does so through an object created by him with his own hands—the work of art.*

René Huyghe, *L'Art et l'Homme*

Virtually every age of civilization has endowed us with magnificent works of art. Among these the most fragile, and therefore the rarest and most moving, are objects made of glass. Yet glass receives only slight attention in the history of art, where it is ranked as a minor form well below the exalted position held by the major arts of painting, sculpture, and architecture. In the light of this tradition, the late 19th century deserves particular credit for its glorious revival of decorative glass, a movement further distinguished by the unprecedented attempt to reconcile what until then had always seemed irreconcilable—the beautiful and the useful.

The resurgence of art glass occurred by reason of several converging trends. The last of the great craftsmen proved capable of especially beautiful work, which the new rich of the bourgeoisie vied with one another to acquire. Dealers, museums, and the great fairs or exhibitions all joined with private collectors in the cultivation of what was a new taste. The *objet d'art* became fashionable. Meanwhile, however, the industrial revolution continued to progress rapidly, transforming the world as it went. Despite the reluctance of traditionalists, society had to acknowledge the new conditions and the needs that had brought them about. As craftsmanship was displaced by standardization, manufacturers sought aesthetic legitimacy through the servile copying of antique models. Industrial capitalism did not create; it exploited found treasure. This simply reinforced the love of pastiches, already sanctioned by the Empress Eugénie's passion for the French 18th century. But hardly had such a trend emerged when certain perceptive critics and collectors began to express concern over the lack of stylistic originality in the fruits of mass production. The Comte de Laborde, for instance, declared that "France must at any cost improve standards through innovation and purify taste by throwing off the routine." Reviewing an exhibition in 1867, a reporter wrote: "From what we produce as art, posterity will think us a capricious nation, at one moment styling ourselves after the Greeks, at another in the manner of the Renaissance, or perhaps on the order of 18th-century boudoirs—while never showing any originality of our own." Terms such as "lethargy," "mechanical reproduction," "insensitivity" appear constantly in the journals of the period, all used to characterize the mediocrity then prevailing in the arts.

Soon, the contradictory demands of industry and aesthetics generated such questions as: Why not create an industrial beauty? Why not invent a new style? The idea can even be traced back as early as 1851. This was the year of the first Universal Exhibition, held in London, when Comte de Laborde, who took charge of the French contribution to the great fair, stated: "The future of the arts, sciences, and industry lies in their cooperation with one another." Then in 1863, with the advice of the writer Prosper Mérimée and with the active promotion of the medievalist-architect-engineer Viollet-le-Duc, both of whom held great power in French political and artistic circles, France mounted her own Universal Exhibition. The underwriters were eleven Parisian industrialists who, calling themselves the Union Centrale des Beaux-Arts Appliqués à l'Industrie, proposed "to support in France the cultivation of those art forms that pursue the realization of beauty in utility . . . to stimulate competition among artists in such work, while popularizing the feeling for beauty and improving public taste."

Next, Philippe de Chenevières, director of the Académie des Beaux-Arts, took the important step of establishing the Ecole des Arts Décoratifs, in addition to a chair in decorative composition at the Académie itself. Finally, in 1882, the Société des Arts Décoratifs and the Union Centrale des Beaux-Arts joined forces to form the Union Centrale des Arts Décoratifs, which resulted in the establishment of the Musée des Arts Décoratifs. Here triumphed all the efforts to harmonize form and function,

7

efforts that now go under the name *design*, which the French call *l'esthétique industrielle*.

The 19th-century movement to rehabilitate the arts and crafts began slowly. It clearly appealed to the handicraft workers themselves, even though they had by then become an anachronism. Viewing the state into which these creative people had fallen, the Goncourt brothers hailed "the unknown, solitary artisan who, while working in a factory tooled by nothing but his fine fingers and two or three basic implements, himself blowing the fire with great waves of a fan, nonetheless tries to express his innermost being."

Inevitably, the machine was resisted first and foremost in England, where industrialization had had the most far-reaching consequences. The critic John Ruskin (1819–1900) undertook a veritable crusade on behalf of a new art that would ensure the ascendancy of man over machine. As the leader of an idealist movement with socialist tendencies, Ruskin founded a museum for workers. "Workers of France and elsewhere," he said, "let us convince men, as best we can, of beauty and goodness."

Heeding the call in England, William Morris (1834–96), a disciple of Ruskin, made an heroic attempt to put his mentor's ideas into practice and thus became the first modern interior designer. Morris wanted to work on even the smallest details of everyday decoration, the better to make beauty combined with utility available to all. Essential to the integrity of his approach was the rediscovery and adoption of traditional tools.

Later, across the Channel, Anatole France would take up the Ruskinian idea. "Art for all," he wrote, "makes life precious and worth living." In France, those who would break with the past and reaffirm the desire for renewal became the founders of what they called *Art Nouveau*. The term itself entered popular usage when Samuel Bing, a fervent promoter of the "new art," made it the name of his gallery-shop at 22 Rue de Provence in Paris.* From there it spread rapidly, for Bing spent a good portion of his fortune to support and help launch what then was an entirely novel style.

The characteristics of the new mode were several. First, quite naturally, came the search for originality and a belief in "the principle that the surest way to stimulate and renew genius is to draw on the traditional sources of inspiration."** This principle found its realization in ornamental schemes based upon the flora and fauna of nature. Thus, again, we find one of the constants of 19th-century civilization, for early in the period the Romantics had sought to rediscover a world of pure sensation and fresh imagination by turning to trees, flowers, and streams. Here, in their flight from civilization, they found their comfort and their refuge. At the end of the century the Symbolists went even further and detected in nature the signs and symbols of subtle correspondence giving access to the invisible. With these the exponents of Symbolism believed they had the means to suggest the ineffable. Also contributing to the Symbolist movement were the poet Charles Baudelaire and the painters Odilon Redon and Gustave Moreau, along with geniuses as dissimilar as the composers Claude Debussy and Richard Wagner. The Symbolists were, furthermore, heirs not only to the Romantics but also to the Pre-Raphaelites, those mid-century English painters and poets whose quest for a personal and original ideal expressed itself through a new and sincere feeling for nature.

The Impressionists too, those optical realists, were concerned with the immaterial—that is, with the play of light, which wraps nature in an ever-changing envelope of at-

---

*Samuel Bing (1838–1903) borrowed the term from the Belgian founders of the *Revue Moderne* who, beginning in 1884, professed their faith in the "new art."

**Emile Bayard. *Le Style Moderne* (Paris, 1919).

mosphere. Like the other schools mentioned here, the Impressionists stood opposed to the materialistic spirit and the stodginess of *petit bourgeois* values.

Art Nouveau, which grew out of all these antecedent and concurrent movements, offered a style wonderfully suited to glass, and the master glassmakers caused it to flower with a grace and a technical virtuosity bordering on the magical.

Two events help place French art glass in historical perspective: the first Impressionist exhibition in 1874; and the Universal Exhibition of 1878, where Emile Gallé's work proved a revelation. On the latter occasion the resemblances between Impressionist painting and Gallé's glass became obvious. Clearly, both the painters and the glassmaker had taken their inspiration from nature, producing works whose forms and colors existed only to give effect to impressions and sensations—"the language of flowers and mute objects," and even the inexpressible "trembling of water on moss."

Eager to escape both their time and their country, artists looked elsewhere for inspiration. One source of satisfaction could be found in the new knowledge of lost civilizations made possible by recent archaeological discoveries in Egypt, Crete, and Italy. Touched by the revived influence from antiquity, glassmakers sought not only to discover the secrets of Egyptian paste glass and Arabian hard enamel, but also to borrow shapes and decorative themes from Persia and Syria. And they seemed to grow hungry for exoticism even as they fed on the new tastes then arriving in the art of the Near and Far East and, especially, in the art of Japan. From 1858, when Japan abolished its feudal system and entered the Meiji era, large numbers of art objects left the great Japanese estates and spread over Europe. Hitherto unknown, these works became the rage, prompting the Goncourts and Henri Cernuschi to form extraordinary collections. Japanese woodcuts captivated the Impressionists, who found a changing, fleeting world similar to their own in the prints of the *ukiyo-e* school. Van Gogh went so far as to say that Japanese art, while fallen into decadence in its own country, had been reborn in France. Since the Japanese sensibility turned easily to nature for inspiration, the defenders of Art Nouveau saw nature as the common point of departure for both the "new art" and the art of Japan. But what particularly amazed the Europeans were the economy of means and the intensity as well as the subtlety of the effects achieved by the Japanese masters. One line, one stroke of the brush could describe or suggest an object, a sensation, or a mood. Without any evident artifice, poetry seemed quite simply to suffuse the scene, drawing the mind into a philosophical or meditative state. It was this, above all, that many Westerners found irresistible.

The wind from the East touched some of the most enterprising glassmakers, prompting them to gain full control over material both malleable and rich in technical possibilities. Meanwhile, imagination and the creative urge became their guides to personal style and new expression. Like the Impressionist painters, the glassmakers opened "the great book of nature." All forms of animal and vegetable life were subject to development as naturalistic, symbolic, or fantastic decoration. Just as the Japanese did, the French glassmakers reconciled beauty and utility, line and decoration, and it is their adventure—their search and discovery—that constitutes the subject of our book.

In the course of this review we shall see why French art glass of this era acquired its original, delicate, and sometimes unusual appearance. By the end of the 19th century art glass had entered households as a familiar part of the décor. Today such objects are collector's pieces. Yet, with their luxuriant, translucent forms, their immaterial and sensitive qualities, they retain the power to evoke the whole atmosphere of that far-off moment—the years around 1900.

1. Auguste Legras. *Chrysanthemum Vase*, c. 1900, height 166 mm/6 1/2″, Kunstmuseum, Coll. Hentrich, Düsseldorf. This piece combines Japanese-type abstract decoration, a flower motif styled after the Art Nouveau manner, and a naturalistic form—the bulb shape. Signed: "Montjoye & Cie.," trademark of Verrerie Legras.

The Technicians
and
the Revival

As the Machine Age progressed through the 19th century, the spirit of stylistic reform joined with the growing demand for decorative objects—seen as status symbols by the socially aspiring bourgeoisie—to encourage a number of glassmakers, both technicians and industrialists, to develop their theoretical and practical knowledge and to perfect their means of expression. Thus, by the final quarter of the period, French makers of decorative glass were in possession of virtually all the techniques known to have been practiced as far back as the Renaissance and even antiquity. At no time in the history of glassmaking had there been so much fruitful research.

But, lacking originality and true creative genius, the technicians were content merely to copy older works or to fashion pastiches based upon them. Their contribution to the rebirth of decorative glass lay in making antique objects and processes a part of everyday experience in the modern atelier. This contribution, however, is not to be disparaged, for by reclaiming the past, it also pointed out, for those who could perceive them, a whole range of new possibilities. One technician of ability was KESSLER, who perfected an economical method of acid engraving (Plate 3bc). After coating a glass piece with bitumen or wax, he used a diamond point to trace a design into the coating and then plunged the piece into acid. Baccarat purchased the process from Kessler in 1863. As a consequence, certain works made by the Kessler method bear the inscription "Procédée Kessler" alongside the Baccarat mark. Other parties, eager to profit from the renewal movement, took up the process purely for commercial exploitation.

Also outstanding among the technicians were the chemists MAES and CLÉMANDOT, who together directed a factory at Clichy. To Clémandot we owe the discovery of crystal made from zinc oxide, which endows glass with brilliancy, great refractiveness, and added elasticity. This artisan, moreover, perfected a method of etching thick glass with hydrofluoric acid vapors (Plate 3a). In 1855 the Maes and Clémandot business held a dominant position in the manufacture of colored crystal.

Thirty years later the Clémandot factory was taken over by LANDIER, who, since 1870, had owned the old Sèvres glassworks on the road to Vaugirard. Founded in the 18th century under Louis XV, the Verrerie de Sèvres was once again active, now in the fabrication of crystal. To develop this business, Landier engaged HOUDAILLE and sponsored extensive research on cut crystal and on enameled, crackled, and aventurine* glass, as well as on the imitation of gemstones. Out of it came the Cristalleries de Sèvres et Clichy Réunies. On September 15, 1885, the firm filed application to patent a new process for decorating both glass and crystal objects.

The Conservatoire des Arts et Métiers has a large selection of Sèvres-Clichy objects. Generally varied in shape, the forms in certain instances reveal a timid effort to break away from the constraints of tradition (Plate 4).

Eventually Houdaille joined forces with an electrical engineer named TRIQUET. Setting up shop at Choisy-le-Roi, the partners applied themselves principally to the use of glass for electric lighting, then a recent but increasingly popular invention. Thanks to their own gifts and to the quality of their production, the glass made by Houdaille and Triquet is compatible, both functionally and aesthetically, with the contemporary style in home furnishings.

*Aventurine glass imitates quartz through the incorporation of large numbers of copper particles held in suspension. The glass must be heated in a way to start the process of crystallization. The making of aventurine glass presents several problems, the chief of which is the need to spread the crystals uniformly throughout the mass. In 1865 Pelouzem discovered that glass with a base of chrome oxide could give the same effect as aventurine glass.

left: 5. Monot et Stumpf. (a) *Imitation rock crystal vase decorated with birds, branches, and grasslike plants,* c. 1880, height 210 mm/8 3/8"; (b) *Yellow pitcher with metallic luster surface, crackled and with thread decoration,* c. 1880, height 210 mm/8 3/8". Musée du Conservatoire des Arts et Métiers, Paris.

below left: 6. Les Frères Boutigny. (a) *Small vase decorated with gold valances and flowering twigs,* c. 1889, height 80 mm/3 1/8". An early use of the process called *intarsia,* whereby the hot "metal" is inlaid with pieces of colored glass. (b) *Crackled-glass vase with applied colored decoration,* c. 1890, height 230 mm/9 1/8". Musée du Conservatoire des Arts et Métiers, Paris.

below right: 7. Monot, Stumpf, Touvier, Viollet & Cie. *Acid-etched and iridescent glass,* c. 1900, Musée du Conservatoire des Arts et Métiers, Paris. Iridescent glass produced with copper vapors in the course of firing became a speciality of this firm. Signed in gold: "Cristallerie de Pantin."

The APPERT brothers, Adrien and Léon, could also be found in Clichy, at 4 Rue des Chasses. They earned a reputation for their clever craftsmanship and expertise in color chemistry, as well as for their production of laboratory, optical, perforated, and reinforced glass. Around 1883 Les Frères Appert advanced the cause of innovation by exhibiting a curious yellow bowl whose decorative clouds were integral with the material the piece was made of. While Emile Gallé took particular account of the Apperts' metallic oxide combinations, both he and Eugène Rousseau benefited from advice offered by the brothers.

In their time the glassware exhibited by the Apperts was held to be in no way inferior to the most beautiful Venetian products (Plate 2). Furthermore, Léon Appert, in collaboration with Jules Henrivaux, was a published authority, having become the author of several important technical treatises.

LES FRÈRES BOUTIGNY were active mostly in Paris between 1880 and 1890. Their work is interesting less for its invention than for its embodiment of diverse techniques. Collectors of the old glass of Bohemia and agents for that nation's modern crystal, they tried to imitate the antique work, even to the perfection of the process of double-layering (casing) glass in different colors. They also produced painted and enameled glassware. Often the Boutignys' glass is crackled,* and the crackled vase now in

*The crackling of glass is a physical phenomenon that occurs when the material is subjected to an abrupt change in temperature. The simplest way to effect this is to take glass in the process of being fused and plunge it into cold water. Crackling can be imitated by rolling the molten glass on a marver that has been covered with broken and crushed glass. An additional firing is needed to fuse the attached pieces to the main mass.

the Conservatoire des Arts et Métiers displays a quality of material and a strength of form all but equal to the audacious work of Auguste Jean (Plate 6).

From 1889 on the Boutigny brothers made their greatest contribution through an *intarsia* technique whereby hot "metal" (glass) is inlaid with pieces of colored glass. A somewhat tentative product of the method, which is akin to casing or double-layering, can be seen in a small vase now in the Conservatoire des Arts et Métiers (Plate 6). Here intarsia serves to create the effect of golden valances, a classical motif of the sort the Boutignys could rarely resist. Once Gallé had taken up intarsia around 1897, he would develop and perfect it with unparalleled authority, calling the process *marqueterie de verre* ("glass marquetry"). Following fashion, the Boutignys also turned out glass enameled in the Arabic manner.

MONOT was a glassmaker who, after service at the Cristallerie de Lyon, set up under his own name at 4 Rue de Thionville in La Villette, an industrial district of Paris. At the Universal Exhibition of 1855 Monot attracted notice with a group of large vases in opaline, a romantic type of glass then much favored. He also displayed objects in white cut glass and some ruby-red glass.

A little later Monot moved to Pantin, another industrial district of Paris, where his son joined the business. Typical of Monot's new, careful workmanship is a vase made in imitation rock crystal and decorated with birds (Plate 5a). Through an original interpretation of Oriental art, this piece reveals a praiseworthy attempt at decorative renewal. For the most part, however, Monot was content to follow Venetian or Bohemian models.

Around 1876 STUMPF joined the Monot firm, which entered an era of prosperity lasting until 1900. Although its technical range was great, the company specialized in opaline glass, as well as in iridescent glass produced by the introduction of copper vapors during firing (Plate 5b). In a published report on the 1878 Universal Exhibition, Didron and Clémandot found the Monot work "of little aesthetic interest, but remarkable for its material, for its imitation of rock crystal, and for its metallized glass in Chinese red."* A flower stand now owned by the Conservatoire des Arts et Métiers offers a good example of a deep and pure red obtained by Monot and Stumpf.

Frequently these masters took their inspiration directly from nature, especially from flowers and animals. At the same time, they also borrowed motifs from the Far East.

Between 1886 and 1888 Monot retired from business, whereupon STUMPF formed a new group with TOUVIER and VIOLLET. The soul of this affair was Touvier, who, according to Henrivaux, became "one of the foremost practitioners in France." The partners went on to produce a great quantity of metallized, iridescent, frosted, and enameled glass (Plate 7), as well as the traditional imitations of gemstones. Industrialists doubling as artists, they also manufactured high-quality sconces and chandeliers.

After 1900 VARREUX succeeded Stumpf and became the new director of the Cristallerie de Pantin. Varreux made glass pieces decorated by means of acid- and wheel-engraved colored layers. Often the motif consisted of pastoral scenes filled with flora and fauna, all composed and detailed with great care. Grisaille shading was used to create an illusion of solid forms in deep space. In all, the decorative quality of the new work proved superior to

anything the firm had produced before. When signing his pieces, Varreux took the pseudonym "de Vez." In such enterprises the marks on glass products changed frequently, even where the director or proprietor remained long with the same firm. For people like Varreux, signatures held little importance. Thus, we find many different marks for the Cristallerie de Pantin, including "Mont Joye."

In 1910 Henrivaux pointed out that the "de Vez" production exhibited at Paris' Musee Galliéra was noteworthy "because of the problems that had been solved and the novelty of the processes used: thick glass, superimposed colors, artistic engraving."

The most important glass manufacturer in France in the period before 1914 was Verreries et Cristallerie de Saint-Denis et des Quatre-Chemins, directed by AUGUSTE LEGRAS, who had begun as a laborer in the plant. It was to his expert leadership that the firm owed its great success. Under Legras the Saint-Denis company absorbed another glassworks, Vidié at Pantin, which made a total payroll of some 1400 workers and 150 decorators.

Altogether, the Legras management produced an impressive number and variety of objects (Plate 8). It literally inundated the market with works notable more for their fantasy than for their artistic qualities. Much sought after were—and still are—the bottles shaped like people, famous buildings, and Bacchus figures. A speciality was the color "Nile green" in a mat finish obtained with acid. The forms are usually simple, but the decoration could often be surrounded with gold. Themes preferred by Legras were the varieties of chrysanthemums, irises, and orchids (Plates 1, 9). Pastel tones also distinguish his production.

Legras practiced every conceivable technique, including frosted glass. He admired Gallé greatly and tried to

*Chinese red, according to technical explanations given by Monot and Stumpf, can be obtained with a mixture of copper and gold inserted and fused between two layers of glass.

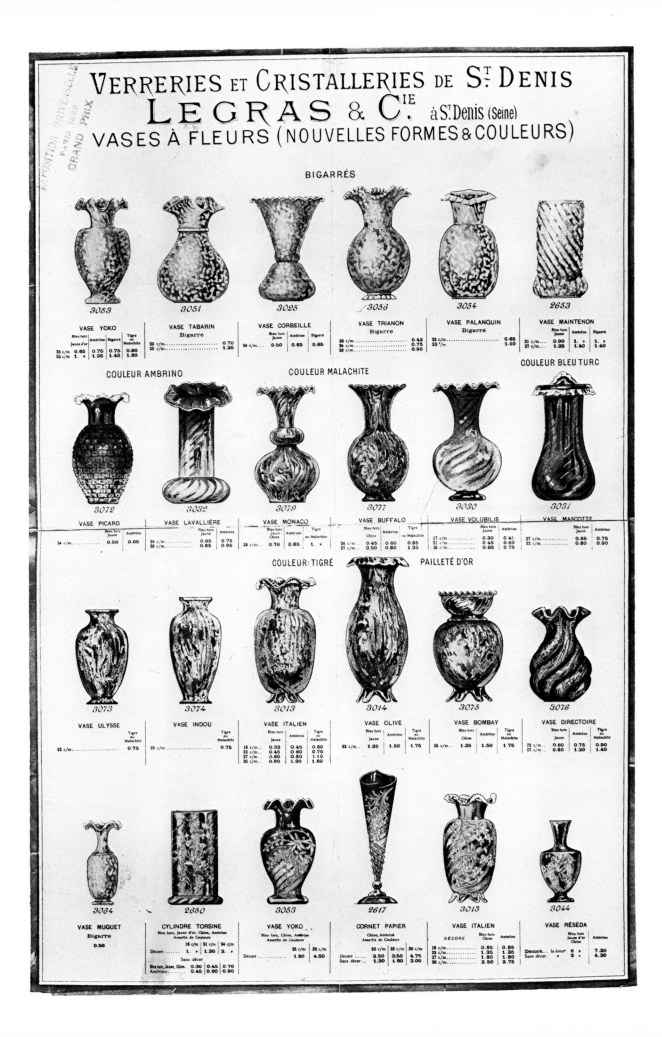

9. Auguste Legras. (a) *Vase with chrysanthemums*, after 1900, height 390 mm/15 3/8″, signed "Legras"; (b) *Vase decorated with mistletoe*, after 1900, height 370 mm/14 5/8″, signed "L Cie St Denis Paris." Kunstmuseum, Coll. Hentrich, Düsseldorf. During the same period the Legras firm used both naturalistic themes inspired by Japanese art and the stylized motifs recommended by Samuel Bing.

imitate him in his more artistic pieces. Unfortunately, the effort yielded little more than weak replicas of the master's work.

The factory at Saint-Denis remained active for fifty years. On the whole its reputation is that of a quality house but one that showed none of the creative verve characteristic of the great glassmakers (Plate 10). The signatures associated with the Saint-Denis operation are "Legras," "Pantin," and "L. à St-Denis."

Vidié at Pantin, before its takeover by Legras, had produced some marbled and veined pieces that, while devoid of great artistic value, have a certain interest (Plate 11). The same could be said of the Mellerio firm at Aubervilliers, which excelled in the fabrication of marbled, silverflecked, iridescent, pearly, or veined glassware in many colors (Plate 12). The Mellerio glass shown at the 1889 Universal Exhibition had generally restrained shapes and received much praise for its sparkle and brilliance. The pieces bear signatures no more frequently than those from Vidié.

Auguste Legras filed many patent applications:

- August 1, 1884, for improving the decoration of bottles and other articles;
- December 17, 1888, for a process of metallizing glass or crystal during the course of manufacture;
- April 2, 1891, for an addition to the glassworker's blowpipe in the form of a pendulum intended to provide mechanical blowing of the glass;
- April 17, 1894, for a process of applying colored flowers, designs, or other motifs to predetermined points on blown glass.

10. Auguste Legras. *Vase with plane-tree leaves*, c. 1900, height 410 mm/16 1/8″, private collection. A classic example of a piece with an acid ground produced industrially. Signed.

11. Vidié et Mellerio. *Marbled vases with several colored layers*, c. 1889, Musée du Conservatoire des Arts et Métiers, Paris. Remarkable technicians, Vidié and Mellerio became part of the vast movement toward aesthetic renewal, making their great contribution in the form of original research on materials and shapes.

12. Joseph Brocard. (a) *Ewer decorated with palmettes, small ornamental flowers, pearls, stems, and flowerets,* c. 1890, height 280 mm/11″, signed; (b) *Bowl decorated with pansies,* c. 1890, diameter 150 mm/5 7/8″; (c) *Beaker decorated with bluets,* c. 1890, height 160 mm/6 3/8″, signed. Musée des Arts Décoratifs, Paris.

Oriental Influences and the Search for New Forms

PHILIPPE-JOSEPH BROCARD (d. 1896)

In any discussion of French art glass, Joseph Brocard must be placed in the first rank among the artists and researchers who in the second half of the 19th century worked to restore glass to the important position it had held in antiquity and the Renaissance.

According to a bulletin distributed in 1874 by the Union Centrale des Arts Décoratifs, Brocard was a restorer and, as the occasion permitted, a collector of objets d'art. Glassmaking itself came to interest him when, after seeing the mosque lamps in the Musée de Cluny, he sought to imitate their magnificent and sumptuous enamels.

Brocard prepared himself through a careful study of all the glassmaking techniques, especially the technique for enamel. An inventive researcher, he was able to reconstruct the hard, colored enamel process in which the Arabs had excelled. This was an achievement, for it is very difficult to attach fusible enamels permanently to glass. The enamels must be hard, and to manufacture them Brocard had to overcome a great many obstacles. "He made," wrote Henrivaux in *Le Verre,* "glass of a special kind and coloration over which he added gilding and enamels. The whole was then fired." Simple though the description may be, the operation remains a problematic and dangerous one. The enamels must fuse at a temperature close to that of glass; otherwise they will not attach solidly to the main mass. Firing may also deform the objects, and to prevent this, it is imperative that temperature and time be carefully controlled. Furthermore, handwork is required to apply designs and to adapt them to the particular surface being decorated.

Brocard began by reproducing mosque lamps and then went on to cups and vases. His lamp imitations were so convincing that contemporaries took them for authentic pieces—actual mosque lamps of the 12th and 13th centuries (Plate 16). Opaque and translucent enamels, gold cabochons, interlaced and arabesque configurations, colors, and even the Kufic inscriptions—all appear in facsimile perfection.

The whole of Brocard's technical prowess was revealed to the public at the Universal Exhibition of 1867. There the artisan exhibited not only shapes derived from Persia, but also traditional shapes, close to Gallo-Roman antiquities and German as well as Italian Renaissance glass. From that time forward, Brocard was considered an innovator in the enameling technique, which became his speciality. With this process he started a fashion later followed by other enamelers, among whom Giboin, Imberton,* Ernie, and Bucan developed much skill but little originality or character (Plate 13). Brocard's talent was acknowledged with a Gold Medal at the 1873 Universal Exhibition in Vienna. Public recognition came again at the 1874 Paris exhibition, where a critic wrote that "he composes and executes blown hanging lamps of his own invention." The work displayed on these occasions seemed to foretell that its creator would free himself from servile imitation of the past. In 1878 he ranked next to Emile Gallé at the Univer-

---

*Imberton had invented a new enameling process that carries his name. In 1884 he gave the Conservatoire des Arts et Métiers a collection of examples showing the successive stages in his technique for applying enamels to glass.

14. Joseph Brocard. *Water-bottle vase enameled with interlaced ornamental foliage,* c. 1890, height 220 mm/8 3/4″, collection F. Marcilhac, Paris. The influence of Islamic art is evident here, but the handles formed as long birds' necks—flamingo or ibis—break the monotony of the flat, abstract patterning of the arabesque décor. Signed.

sal Exhibition. Didron, then a reporter, noted in Brocard's work "a remarkable grasp of the Eastern sense of color and decoration" (Plate 13a).

In the early 1880s, however, Brocard may have come under the influence of Gallé, for he moved towards a greater naturalism, suppressing the friezes and arabesques of his first period in favor of floral themes treated with greater freedom (Plate 12). Now Brocard found inspiration in pansies, orchids, bluets, mistletoe, satinflowers—all native to the Art Nouveau repertory. He even dared to make a pansy-decorated cup the instrument of a tender message: *A Elle je pense* (Plate 12b). The technician had become a poet, or the poet a technician, in order to express his feelings with simple delicacy. Brocard's increasingly personal inspiration led him to stylize certain decorations, even going beyond the tendencies of the period. Thus, on classical Gallo-Roman shapes, copied in 1885 from a cabochon beaker in the Musée de Saint-Germain-en-Laye, his satinflower or mistletoe designs have a compositional rhythm that seems to anticipate the formal rigor of the 1925 style. Brocard's classicized beaker also became a pretext for a decoration of bluets created with a play of lines that is absolutely modern (Plate 12c).

Beginning in 1884, Brocard's son Emile became a collaborator. Was it at this time that Brocard *père* lived at 23 Rue Bertrand in Paris, or well before? No known document gives exact dates. The signature then became "Brocard et Fils," most often engraved in gold.

Joseph Brocard died in 1896, and from about that time, up to the turn of the century, his studios continued their production under the name of Verrerie Brocard. Shortly after 1900, however, the firm disappeared.

15. Joseph Brocard. *Cup enameled with ornamental foliage, branches, thistles, and the cross of Lorraine,* c. 1878–84, height 90 mm/3 1/2″, collection F. Marcilhac, Paris. The decorative details date this piece after the 1878 Universal Exhibition, which put Brocard in touch with the artist-glassmakers of Nancy, especially Émile Gallé.

16. Joseph Brocard. *Small mosque lamp with enameled decoration on a gold-lustered ground,* 1878, height 200 mm/7 7/8″, Musée du Verre, Charleroi. This piece represents a small-scale imitation of mosque lamps of the 13th and 14th centuries. Here Brocard also imitated the ancient enameling techniques of Arabic Islam.

On the whole, Brocard was a technician rather than a creator. This must be said, for despite several decorative discoveries, it was his Arabic or Persian enameled glass that, above all else, had an impact on contemporary France. A man of taste, Brocard is distinguished for his technical research, his elegant shapes, the correctness of his proportions, and his decorative grace. He knew how to choose his models and how to use them in the creation of a homogeneous oeuvre (Plates 14,15,17).

Even if Brocard was stylistically limited, his importance is undeniable, mainly in the new life he gave to the art of enameled glass, and in the very real influence he had on Emile Gallé, on the brothers Auguste and Antonin Daum, as well as on a good many other artists (Plate 20).

17. Joseph Brocard. *Glass enameled with ornamental foliage and arabesques,* c. 1885, height 160 mm/6 3/8", collection F. Marcilhac, Paris. Although formed like a 16th-century German tankard, this glass evokes through the richness of its decoration the luxury of Oriental palaces.

Abstract of the patent application for a new process of applying enamels to glass and foil:

1. We begin by preparing translucent or transparent enamels in the various colors that will be needed in order to carry out our design. The enamels must have the same fusibility as the glass they are to decorate, so that the enamels and the glass are "in accord" with one another (that is, behave in a similar manner during firing) and thus resist cracking. Once the enamels have been made ready, we pick them up with a brush and then apply them either in intaglio grooves or inside cloisons of gold or of vitrifiable colors. Thus prepared, the piece is placed in the kiln and fired until the enamels have been completely fused.

2. For enamels on foils of gold, silver, platinum, or copper, we start by cutting the foil to fit the planned design. Then, with the enamels prepared as indicated above, we apply them with translucent or transparent enamel fluxes in the various colors required for the desired effect. When this has been done, we apply the precut foils to the liquid enamels. We allow the whole to dry, and then on top of the foil we make a new application of enamel, this time a translucent enamel, either colored or colorless. With this operation accomplished, we place the piece in the kiln and fire it until all the enamels have fused. It is equally possible to surround the enamels with gold, with platinum, or with vitrifiable colors, or simply apply them without a cloison or container of any kind.

3. For either translucent or transparent enamels under translucent enamel, we use the following procedure: Once the enamels have been prepared as explained above and the design has been made ready on the piece to be worked—that is, outlined by drawing or with cloisons—we prepare translucent or transparent enamels for the required colors and apply them to the glass as required by the design. Next, we allow the whole to dry and then cover the piece, in whole or in part depending on the design, with translucent or transparent enamel.

4. For brush painting on enamel, we first apply to the glass, as a general ground, a colored or colorless enamel, or we dust directly onto the glass oxide colorants that we then apply to the ground with a drawing instrument or a brush. Thereafter we cover the piece with translucent enamel and fire the whole to the point of complete fusion.

5. Translucent or transparent enamels imitating precious stones. The enamels come about like those described in Paragraph 1, but the foils are independent of the enamels—that is, instead of being placed directly under the enamel, or sandwiched between two layers of enamel, as described in Paragraph 2, they are applied on the side of the glass opposite that receiving the enamel, which means that separating the foil and the enamel is the thickness of the glass to which they have been applied.

6. The procedures we have just described are applicable to all sorts of glass: clear or colored, plate glass, strass, etc., whatever the dimensions of the piece to be decorated, and whatever the form, flat, cylindrical, or yet otherwise. We can, according to the circumstance, vary the proportions of the several elements employed.

In sum, we claim as our exclusive and absolute property, in whole as well as in part, the diverse procedures that we have here described.

Paris, August 20, 1891
P. pon de MM.P.J. Brocard et F.E. Brocard

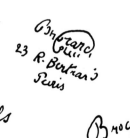

AUGUSTE JEAN

Auguste Jean first came to notice around 1860 as a ceramist and faïence decorator who followed Italian and French Renaissance models. Using Faenza and Limoges enamels as his favorite sources, he gained experience that would prove very useful when later he turned to art glass.

For his first glass pieces, Jean employed the fashionable hard enamels inspired by Oriental glassmakers. Like the young Gallé, Jean enameled on white crystal, but the free placement and interlace of his floral patterns immediately disclosed the sensibility of a faïence decorator (Plate 18). They also revealed a desire for innovation. A good example of Jean's work in the 1880s is the cylindrical vase owned by the Conservatoire des Arts et Métiers (Plate 19b). Both in its classical form and in its novel plasticity, which Jean effected with pincers while the metal was hot, the piece anticipates its creator's future works.

The strong and attractive personality present in Jean's work triumphed at the Universal Exhibition of 1878. Abandoning enamels in the Persian manner, the glassmaker showed vases with highly original, even bold and spectacular shapes, in which he seemed quite at ease in expressing himself. And the material alone proved sufficient as an expressive means and no longer required decoration. An orchid vase in blue crystal evinces Jean's technical skill in its dynamic extensions (Plate 19a). Imbued with the same spirit is the astonishing "globe with vaporous waves," also in the Conservatoire des Arts et Métiers.

To show that he was not impervious to the artistic influences of his own time, Jean looked to Japanese models and made a delightful mauve bottle whose pure shape gleams with an iridescence created by silver foil fused between two layers of glass (Plate 19c). It is the ideal piece for an

aesthete, offering much satisfaction in its simplicity. This rare experiment proves that Jean knew, when necessary, how to make works in perfect harmony with the mood and manner of the Far East.

Thanks to their originality, Jean's forms and shapes had a deserved success. They certainly helped open new perspectives and to liberate glassmaking artists from the shackles of tradition.

Most of Auguste Jean's known pieces are in Paris at the Conservatoire des Arts et Métiers. Usually they are signed.

18. Auguste Jean. *Vase enameled with flowers and birds*, c. 1878, height 300 mm/11 3/4″, collection S. Deschamps, Paris. The artist's talent is shown less in the quality of the enamels than in the originality of their application in bold relief.

below: 19. Auguste Jean. (a) *Orchid vase*, c. 1882, height 200 mm/7 7/8″, signed; (b) *Vase decorated with flowers*, c. 1882, height 280 mm/11″, signed; (c) *Bottle vase with silver foil*, c. 1882, height 220 mm/8 3/4″. Musée du Conservatoire des Arts et Métiers, Paris. The blue-crystal flower vase is a brilliant exercise in style, showing the remarkable effects Jean could obtain in materials alone. By contrast, the bottle on the right evokes the purity of shape and the sobriety of Japanese art. A more characteristic form is the cylindrical vase at the center, for which Jean gave free rein to his fantasy in designing the decoration.

right: 20. Ernie. *Enameled glass*, c. 1880, height 180 mm/7 1/8″, Musée des Arts Décoratifs, Paris. The influence of Brocard is evident in the enameling technique.

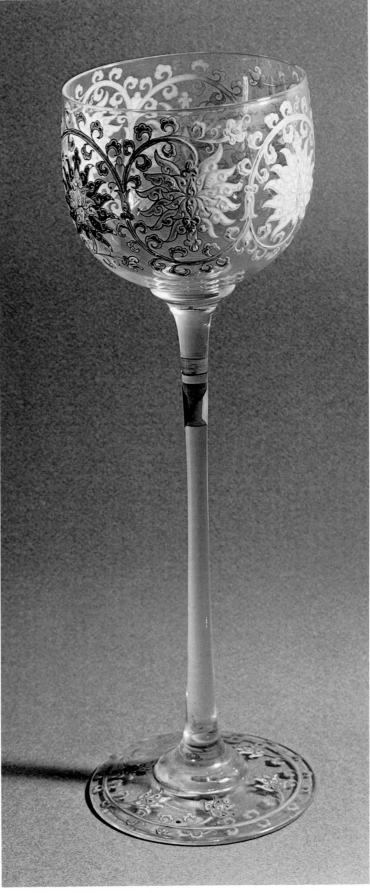

above: 21. Eugène Rousseau. (a) *Brush holder decorated in intaglio with a Japanese-style landscape*, c. 1890, height 170 mm/6 5/8", signed "Rousseau et Léveillé"; (b) *Crackled-glass ewer with colored occlusions*, c. 1885, height 255 mm/ 10". Collection A. Lesieutre, Paris. This last piece, inspired by German Renaissance shapes, could be attributed either to Rousseau or to Léveillé, since they both worked from the same model.

left: 22. Eugène Rousseau. (a) *Vase with long neck, intaglio-engraved with cherry blossoms*, c. 1885, height 250 mm/9 3/4"; (b) *Vase decorated with a cloud-filled landscape, intaglio-engraved*, c. 1885, height 200 mm/7 7/8". Musée des Arts Décoratifs, Paris. These two vases show all that Rousseau owed to Japanese art, in shape, in theme, in decorative style, and even in material, which imitates hard stones.

23. Eugène Rousseau. (a) *Smoked crystal jug,* height 153 mm/6″; (b) *Small vase decorated with intercalary (inserted) trees,* height 215 mm/8 1/2″; (c) *"Wiederkomm" beaker engraved with peacock plumes,* height 262 mm/ 10 3/8″; (d) *Vase in crackled and colored glass, with a relief of chimeras,* height 260 mm/10 1/4″. Musée du Conservatoire des Arts et Métiers, Paris. These four unsigned pieces were given to the museum by Rousseau in 1884. Some were inspired by the German Renaissance, others by Japanese art.

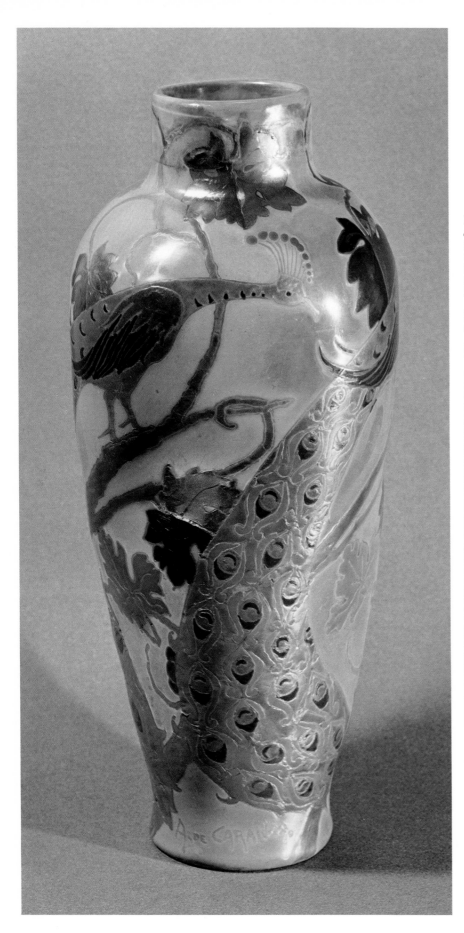

left: 24. Amédée de Caranza. *Vase with peacocks and flowers,* c. 1898, height 330 mm/13″, private collection. While the curves of a motif inspired by Mozarabic faïences adapt themselves beautifully to the piece's shape, the quality of the enamel used for coloring the motif receives enhancement from the lustered ground. Signed, under the foot in red: "Noyon 628"; on the base: "A. de Caranza."

below: 25. Amédée de Caranza. *Vase decorated with a boxwood branch,* c. 1895, height 151 mm/5 7/8″, Musée des Arts Décoratifs. The discovery of Japanese art led the artist to this degree of simplicity. Signed.

FRANÇOIS-EUGÈNE ROUSSEAU (1827–91)

A major artist in his time, François-Eugène Rousseau occupies a distinguished place in the history of glassmaking. He began as a porcelain and crystal merchant, located at 41 Rue Coquillère in Paris, and first demonstrated his artistic capacity in 1867, when he had a porcelain table service made from a design by Félix Bracquemond. Since Bracquemond was among the earliest of the European enthusiasts of Japanese art, the work he did for Rousseau inevitably reflects the spare aesthetic of the Far East.

Some years later, still inspired by Japanese art, Rousseau had his own designs applied by intaglio on clear or lightly colored glass. They are either simply engraved or enameled with decorations in the Korean manner—that is, with butterflies or insects delicately placed on branches of cherry blossom. After obtaining the glass from the Appert brothers' factory in Clichy, Rousseau arranged for it to be engraved by two very gifted collaborators: Eugène Michel and Alphonse-Georges Reyen. "Not a shaper of materials, yet a craftsman," is how Garnier characterized Rousseau in 1886 (*La Verrerie au XIXe Siècle*). His strength lay in intuition and a compositional rigor that brought out the best in the talents of others.

Such was Rousseau's comprehension of the infinite possibilities of glass that he even learned to derive aesthetic benefit from the slashes of dark coloration caused in light-toned vases by firing accidents. More important, Rousseau was one of the first to take up the manufacture of overlay or cased glass made with two or three differently colored layers. In doing so he revived a technique known to the Venetians and the Chinese in the 18th century. And this took place at a moment when Gallé was still decorating monochrome glass. In its glyptic or cold state, Rousseau had the superficial layer (overlay) of opaque, and often intensely colored, glass carved as if it were stone (Plate 22). In passages where this occurred, he revealed the under layer of glass, and since this foundation had been left translucent, the effects obtained by the casing and the carving were both bold and refined. Most of all, the process yielded a distinct sense of sculptural relief.

At the Universal Exhibition of 1878 public and critics alike took great interest in Rousseau's latest novelties. These were imitations of gemstones—sardonyx, agate—meant to rival the rock crystals of the Far East. To conceal the glass' true character, even the natural imperfections of real stone were simulated. The effect was obtained through interior localized oxidizations, which enlivened cloudy or sparkling glass with a wonderful and unexpected marbling (Plate 23d).

Rousseau also exhibited molded glass, engraved with flowers or landscapes in the Japanese style and covered with enameled painting. The "bamboo" vase of 1878 is a beautiful example, the middle part soberly engraved and enameled on a double layer of glass (Plate 26).

Rousseau knew no chemistry; thus, his technical collaboration with the Appert brothers became increasingly important. The results of their research into materials made a great sensation at the 1884 exhibition of the Union des Arts Appliqués. Like Gallé, Rousseau triumphed with his famous crackled vases imitating veined quartz and even strass, with its jewellike brilliance (Plate 23d). Louis de Fourcaud was right when he wrote that Rousseau "possesses to a supreme degree the sense of the precious in

glassmaking." Crackled glass, his most characteristic production, is obtained by immersing the hot object in cold water between two firings. The harsh cooling causes a network of sparkling cracks to form. A technique borrowed from 16th-century Venice, it was used for a Rousseau vase ornamented with a richly plastic pair of chimeras. In the same piece the intensely colored upper layer has been selectively removed to disclose a rabbit hiding in the translucent ground layer (Plate 27).

Attracted by the refinement of the Renaissance, Rousseau also exhibited a series of opulently contoured ewers based upon German goldsmiths' work of the 16th century (Plate 21b). These rarely signed pieces may have been executed under the direction of Ernest Léveillé, Rousseau's pupil and, from 1885, his successor.

By 1884 the Rousseau imitations of gemstones were better, more perfect than ever, for the engraver had become a true master of his art. The Musée des Arts Décoratifs owns, for example, two vases that represent a brilliant interpretation of Japanese art. The inner layer of the one in Plate 22b advances unexpectedly, punctuating the lyrical landscape inspired by Fuji-Yama. Rousseau's taste for strongly accented relief is evident in the services he created in the Bohemian or Venetian style. For his tall cornets inspired by German 17th–18th-century *Wiederkomm* glass,

26. Eugène Rousseau. *"Bamboo" vase, engraved and enameled with bamboo leaves, tropical creepers, and arabesques,* 1878, height 400 mm/15.5/8″, collection J.-Cl. Brugnot, Paris. One can understand the enthusiasm that greeted the appearance of such vases at the 1878 Universal Exhibition. Here Rousseau revealed how well he had assimilated the Japanese art that was then so much the fashion. Signed.

made for taking an *au revoir* or "goodbye" drink of wine or beer, he preferred the simple, broad design of a peacock plume (Plate 23c) or a chrysanthemum on a ground of ornamental foliage or of arabesques gilded and stippled with enamel. His technical research led him to incorporate metallic filaments in improvised designs.

From 1885 Rousseau was associated with Léveillé. Works the two friends made in collaboration bear conjoined signatures. They also carry the mark of Japanese influence, as in the paintbrush holder decorated with motifs taken from a print by Hiroshige, with Fuji-Yama in the background (Plate 21a).

Very rarely do works attributed to Rousseau alone carry his stamp. It is therefore only through stylistic similarities to the signed pieces in museums or private collections that identification can be made.

Rousseau's greatest contribution lay in turning ancient techniques to new purposes, and in assimilating the lessons of China and Japan, all the while shaping these influences with his own personal intuition. Lines are simple, but never dry or harsh. His works differ from Gallé's in their very spareness, for Rousseau sought only those effects that could be gained from the material itself. He quite simply began France's artistic renewal in glass and modern glassmaking.

27. Eugène Rousseau. *Crackled and colored vase with chimeras in relief and a rabbit in a landscape,* c. 1885, height 260 mm/10 1/8″, collection A. Lesieutre, Paris. Louis de Fourcaud, speaking about the artist's sumptuous material, said that Rousseau "possesses to a supreme degree the sense of the precious in glassmaking."

AMÉDÉE DE CARANZA

Born in Istanbul, Amédée de Caranza went to work in France at a very young age. He was a complete artist, as much a musician as a painter, and an excellent decorator of both faïence and glass.

Around 1870 Caranza entered the faïence works of Longwy, directed by the brothers Fernand and Hippolyte d'Huart. Under their guidance, the concern took on fresh life, thanks mainly to the installation of a new design studio, which began using cloisonné enamels in the Japanese manner. The artistic management is attributed to Amédée de Caranza, who in 1875, however, left the atelier at Longwy for that of Jules Vieillard in Bordeaux, a firm directed after the founder's death in 1868 by his sons, Charles and Albert. Failing in their efforts to advance the operation, the Vieillards called on Amédée de Caranza to take over the creation of the artistic pieces, which were inspired by Moorish or Japanese art and called "enamels." In this production lay the Vieillards' hope for the development of their firm.

But some time later Caranza left them too and went to work for Clément Massier at Vallauris in the south of France. A specialist in the use of metallic lusters on faïence, Massier had real impact on the later glass produced by Caranza. Indeed, it was thanks to Massier that Caranza found a new stimulus in Hispano-Moorish faïence, which is characterized by ornamental motifs with dynamic and elegant curves, as well as by the harmonious integration of forms and décor. This can be seen in the handsome peacock vase reproduced in Plate 24.

Next, from 1890 to about 1914, the peripatetic Caranza was at Noyon, in Oise, with Henri Copillet's firm, where he became a brilliant collaborator, specializing in the creation of beautiful art glass.

Copillet, for his part, was the printer of *Le Libéral*, a newspaper with offices in the Place de l'Hôtel-de-Ville in Noyon. Around 1900 Copillet moved his printing shop to the Paris road. There, finding a huge studio with a furnace, he decided to make it available to some artists, including Amédée de Caranza. Copillet was also director of the Brass and Reed Band of Noyon, which was very successful, thanks to the talents of artist-musicians working with him. Among the latter, one again finds Amédée de Caranza, whose musical and glassmaking abilities Copillet greatly appreciated.

Because their glass studio and archives were destroyed during World War I, no written trace remains of the efforts of Copillet and Caranza. Works signed with both names are the only evidence of their collaboration. But these are very decorative pieces, with metallic reflections and a close resemblance to ceramics. Whether simulating the winding course of water, the flight of clouds, the silvery reflections of the satinflower, or the sumptuous plumage of a peacock, Amédée de Caranza is unrivaled in the way he made his designs iridescent, using fire alone and foregoing all reworking or retouching. Each piece was complete as soon as it had cooled. A fine example is the vase reproduced in Plate 25.

In 1902 Caranza joined with Madame Duc to file a patent application for "the decoration of electric light bulbs and, in a general way, for all kinds of pieces in glass, crystal, or other transparent materials." This is the process with which Caranza obtained his famous metallic luster,

and the patent application, providing a full, technical description, is reproduced here. High quality works, Caranza's pieces have traditional shapes and ornamentation derived from the aquatic or floral themes familiar to Art Nouveau. And the master knew well how to give them freshness and vitality, as can be seen in the cylindrical vase illustrated in Plate 28.

Also calling on Caranza to create art glass in his own new style was Devore Salviati, whose Venetian factory participated, from 1864, in the first movements toward a revival of fine art glass.

It was in the same spirit that Edouard de Neuville worked with Copillet, a collaboration that probably involved Caranza. De Neuville's signed works are in a similar style.

Amédée de Caranza stamped his objects in either copper red or gold. After the patent application, some pieces were marked "Duc de Caranza."

28. Amédée de Caranza. *Vase with tropical creepers*, after 1900, height 154 mm/6 1/8″, collection Lecuyer, Brussels. While remaining faithful to Art Nouveau themes, Caranza moved gradually towards the more symmetrical and less organic forms soon to be favored.

Abstract of a patent application:

To make our new process understood, we will give an example:

Let us take an ordinary electric light bulb. On its surface we execute a decoration with a certain number of different metal oxides. These oxides can be applied with water, with oil, with gum arabic, and, in principle, with almost any appropriate liquid or semiliquid substance.

The bulb thus decorated is placed in a kiln and then fired in the way normally used for glass, crystal, or opaline, but, in that firing, we force the oxides to lose their oxygen so that they return to their original metal state. To effect this reduction, we introduce before, during, or after the firing any suitable reductive material, such as coal, oil, carbide, hydrogen, heating gas either pure or mixed with air, and that in a quantity sufficient to complete the reduction.

Instead of proceeding in a kiln, as described above, we can subject the piece, after it has been decorated with metallic oxides, to the flame of a blowpipe, a gas jet, or any other apparatus providing heat sufficient to reduce the oxides.

This treatment can be effected during or after the fabrication of the piece in glass, crystal, or opaline.

Paris, May 10, 1902
P.P. de Mme J. Duc, née Descôtes et M.A. Caranza

29. Haraut-Guignard. *A pair of silver-mounted vases in engraved crystal, with a mythological decoration representing Amphytrite and Neptune,* c. 1902, height 220 mm/8 5/8″, collection M. Prouvé, Nancy. Signed with the interlaced letters "HG" followed by "Le Rosey Paris."

The Successors to François-Eugène Rousseau

ERNEST-BAPTISTE LÉVEILLÉ

For Léveillé, we have neither a birth nor a death date, only the information that he was born in Paris, and that from 1869 he was in charge of a retail shop at 74 Boulevard Haussmann specializing in glass and porcelain. Interested in the technology of materials, he became first the pupil of Eugène Rousseau, then his collaborator, and finally his associate in 1885. Like Rousseau, Léveillé loved to combine acid engraving with the engraving wheel. In addition, he knew all the advantages to be drawn from glass overlaid in different colors and engraved after firing. Here he invariably took his guide from Oriental art. For all these reasons, Rousseau happily entrusted Léveillé with the direction of the firm, beginning in 1888.

Léveillé also collaborated with Eugène Michel, and for the Universal Exhibition of 1889 the two prepared crackled glass in yellows and reds, which they obtained by adding uranium or copper oxides to the metal. Léveillé continued to use marbling, along with imitations of gems and veined quartz, while still making gold insertions (Plate 30). Some double-layered or cased glass of lively color (usually red) on a neutral ground is wheel-engraved with animals, aquatic plants, or flowers (Plate 31). Occasionally, however, the form is simply modeled and then adorned with a bamboo branch to evoke the Far East. The casing is sometimes turned back on itself, producing shading and a variety of effects. After the example of Rousseau, Léveillé made the models and then had them executed and engraved according to very precise instructions. With these excellent works he won a Gold Medal.

Critics, however, found Léveillé's shapes more severe than those of Gallé and Reyen. This was because Léveillé, instead of searching for new shapes, preferred to create his effects by means of an ornamentation that depended upon color or upon the qualities inherent in the material itself. After 1890, however, the shapes assumed a new strength (Plates 34–37). Worked and distorted by hand, or with the pincers, while still hot, they became more asymmetrical, which was fully in keeping with the new tendencies of the period. Léveillé also liberated the curves and arabesques of his decoration, and specialized in sinuous lines and spirals applied by intaglio or carved in relief. Rousseau, by comparison, displayed greater vivacity and more brilliance, but also a less profound inspiration.

Léveillé showed regularly at the Salons and other exhibitions. In 1892 he again offered colored crystal with several engraved layers. During the following years, he went on to exhibit imitations of jade, agate, and strass, enhanced with sparkling fissures. He also brought forth engravings inspired by Renaissance cameos, in a material easily mistaken for cornelian. The Musée des Arts Decoratifs has a fine example.

Finally, Léveillé won another Gold Medal, this time at the Universal Exhibition of 1900, where his vigorous reliefs and capricious, unexpected details were much admired. Some crackled vases have as many as three layers of glass and are so deeply engraved that their decoration of swamp-grown, wind-blown reeds seems in places to have the three-dimensionality of a bas-relief (Plate 37).

After 1900 Léveillé took over Paris' Toy firm, at 10 Rue de la Paix. There, in addition to his personal production, he made table services in white or tinted glass, engraved in several layers and signed "Toy & Léveillé." A little later

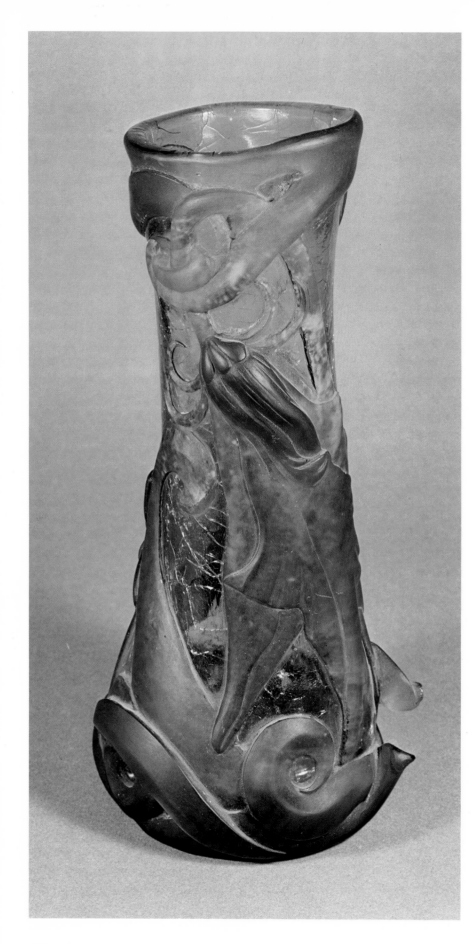

left: 32. Eugène Michel. *Vase decorated with gourd leaves and stems,* c. 1900, height 273 mm/10 5/8″, Musée des Arts Décoratifs, Paris. A true glass sculpture, this highly original work illustrates Michel's engraving talent, as well as his taste for lushly decorative themes worked in rich, plastic relief. Like his teacher, Rousseau, Michel loved to associate crackled backgrounds with engraving. Signed.

below: 33. Eugène Michel. *Vase decorated with waterlilies and reeds,* c. 1895, height 260 mm/10 1/8″, collection Lespine, Paris. In this work of Japanese inspiration, the different layers of colored glass give effect to a movement of water and reeds. Signed.

far left: 34. Ernest Léveillé. *Crackled vase, twisted and marbled,* c. 1890, height 270 mm/10 5/8″, private collection. Intaglio-carved spirals are among the forms distinctive of Léveillé's work. They allow him to accentuate the shape of the vase. Signed.

left: 35. Ernest Léveillé. *Vase decorated with foliage,* c. 1895, height 203 mm/8″, Kunstmuseum, Coll. Hentrich, Düsseldorf. The intaglio-carved spirals of the preceding vase are here replaced with a silver armature signed by Guerchet, one of the best goldsmiths then practicing in Paris.

the firm was absorbed by Léveillé's successors, the glass-makers Haraut-Guignard (Plate 29). The interlaced letters "H" and "G" constitute a new mark, sometimes appearing side by side with the name of the sales outlet: Le Rosey in Paris. The business remained faithful to the impetus first given by Rousseau and carried on by Léveillé.

Some vases made before 1890 carry the juxtaposed signatures of Rousseau and Léveillé; then, after Rousseau had turned the business over to his associate, that of Léveillé alone.

E. Leveille
E. Rousseau Paris

E. Leveille
E Rousseau
Paris

E. Léveillé

HG

right: 36. Ernest Léveillé. *Vase in the form of a bamboo stem,* c. 1895, height 140 mm/5 1/2″, collection F. Marcilhac, Paris. Léveillé has translated the very form of the bamboo stem into glass, exploiting a Japanese theme to its ultimate limit.

far right: 37. Ernest Léveillé. *Vase with floral decoration,* c. 1890, height 195 mm/7 5/8″, Kunstmuseum, Coll. Hentrich, Düsseldorf. Léveillé has applied a floral decoration in deep relief onto a crackled ground. He differs from Rousseau in the greater vigor and plasticity of his decorative designs. Intaglio-signed: "Léveillé Paris."

43

EUGÈNE MICHEL

A very gifted artist, Eugène Michel has left little information about either his personal life or his relatively small production. To know him at all, we must seek out the rare signed pieces now preserved in a few private and public collections.

We know, at least, that Michel was born at Lunéville in Lorraine, and that around 1867–68 he worked as an engraver and decorator, first for Eugène Rousseau and then for Rousseau's successor, Léveillé. Michel seems to have become independent around 1890, when he exhibited double-layered glass and engraved crystal vases in vivid reds and greens, striped with runs of blue, on an uncolored or opaline ground.

Like Rousseau, Michel specialized in crackled glass, with several differently colored layers cut deeply so as to give an effect of amplitude and breadth. Such a work can be seen in a vase belonging to the Musée de Arts Décoratifs; it has a crackled ground and the shape of a truncated cone around which wind volutes and a gourd stem with appliquéd leaves (Plate 32). Very individual is the vase decorated with waterlilies carved in high relief, with the movement of the pond and reeds visible through the successive strata of engraved glass superimposed upon a unified ground (Plate 33). Michel had so mastered the technique of engraving that even on uncolored or monochrome glass or crystal of considerable thickness he could, through deep engraving alone, create a floral decoration of great purity and refinement. The character of his artistry is richly evident in Plate 38.

Because of the dearth of examples, Michel's work is difficult to judge as a whole, but he seems to have been influenced mainly by his master François-Eugène Rousseau, by Japanese art, and by the multilayered Chinese glass of the 18th and 19th centuries. His shapes are simple, but not monotonous; often they are slightly flared at the top and then reinforced with a decorative design that is well adapted to the shape, as in Oriental art.

38. Eugène Michel. *Vase with engraved decoration of aquatic plants*, c. 1895–1900, height 225 mm/8 7/8″, Kunstmuseum, Coll. Hentrich, Düsseldorf. Excellent engraving typifies Eugène Michel's style, especially where the movemented decoration stands in marked contrast to the sober shape of the vase. Signed.

Along with Rousseau and Gallé, Eugène Michel may be considered one of the artist-glassmakers who best assimilated the art of the Far East into his own personality, and best transformed and stylized nature through a sumptuous material. His works are signed in diamond point.

N.B. Eugène Michel should not be confused with a Nancy glassmaker of the same name, whose much inferior talent was devoted to landscape decorations, applied in grisaille and in the style of minor landscape painters.

ALPHONSE-GEORGES REYEN

Alphonse-Georges Reyen became known a little after 1870 as an engraver and delicate colorist of stained glass. Then, working for Emile Gallé, he began to specialize in both wheel and acid engraving. Describing his method, he wrote: "The white vase is covered with light layers of superimposed enamels in different colors, so as to present a flat, unified surface. First, the design is traced, and then, by very lightly attacking the colors needed for the design, different colors are gradually produced, with tonalities of differing intensities and with powerful contrasts of light and shade, all standing out against the solid white glass that provides the transparency. This is very difficult and complicated work, demanding a great sureness of hand to obtain an artistic effect." A classical technique, it produces infinitely varied effects, thanks to the multiple combinations of colors and designs.

Around 1877 Reyen attracted the attention of Eugène Rousseau and became one of the latter's most gifted collaborators. This fortunate union helped improve Reyen's technique; it also oriented him towards new fields of inquiry. At the Universal Exhibition of 1889, he offered on his own account some very beautiful overlay or cased vases enameled and then engraved with the wheel. According to Jules Henrivaux, their "perfect cutting—fine, regular, and brilliant—gives an effect comparable to cameos in gemstones."

Following Rousseau's lead, Reyen created decorations that are brilliant, Japanese-inspired re-creations in glass of such flora and fauna as blossoms, grasses, seaweed, insects, birds, and fish (Plate 41). A vase ornamented with a woman reclining among branches is in the fashion of Art Nouveau's characteristic flower-woman. But the vase shapes remained classical and traditional, since it was engraving alone that held the artist's interest. Meanwhile, Reyen continued his early fascination with the art of stained glass, showing in 1889 a window decorated with nymphs running across rocks.

Setting up business on his own at 17 Boulevard de Solférino in the Paris suburb of Rueil, Reyen pursued his research and achieved a style of engraving that gained increasing depth, actually creating shadows that throw the design into relief, in clearly distinct tones, on glass of two, three, or even four layers. With this new mastery of technique, he produced a brown grisaille vase, whose decoration of two cattle drinking recalls a Barbizon painting, both in the quality of the graduated spatial recession and in the nuances of brown. This work can be seen in the Conservatoire des Arts et Métiers. In 1893 Reyen submitted to the Société Nationale des Beaux-Arts three very beautiful vases, in which the techniques of acid etching and wheel engraving are combined on cased glass, resulting in a decoration of poppies that stands out in clear relief against a field of grasses (Plate 42b). With equal success, Reyen took up a new technique—that of intercalary or inserted decoration—which is exemplified in the charming vase now belonging to the Musée des Arts Décoratifs (Plate 42a). Here we can see flying insects upon a background of engraved plants and ears of grain, the whole realized in delicate, naturalistic colors.

Reyen received a medal at the Universal Exhibition of 1900, by which time he had evolved a new method and obtained highly original effects through the use of enamel upon an imperfectly purified glass called "malfin." In his account of the 1900 show, Edouard Garnier praised "the suppleness and grace with which the flowers are drawn and cut."

Among the vases Reyen offered at this time, some are enhanced with a bronze mount, which adds to their precious quality. His varied appliqués of material and his decorative taste—neither vulgar nor pretentious—make this master an artist of great orginality.

The most important works by Alphonse-Georges Reyen date from the beginning of the century. They are usually signed in wheel engraving.

right: 39. Les Frères Pannier. *Parrot Vase*, c. 1888, height 235 mm/ 9 1/4", Musée des Arts Décoratifs, Paris. Despite the sharply contrasted, intense colors, the work remains harmonious, with the beak and talons gilded. The drama of the piece comes from the carving away of successive layers of glass, a wheel process through which the decoration was created—or found—within the several strata of cased or overlaid glass. Signed in diamond point.

below: 40. Les Frères Pannier. This detail of the vase reproduced in Plate 39 demonstrates the kind of effect that can be obtained by wheel engraving. Strong relief allows the parrot's head to stand forth in red, while the plumage takes on the pale green revealed in the lowest underlayer of glass.

LES FRÈRES PANNIER

The name Pannier is associated with L'Escalier de Cristal ("The Crystal Staircase"), a firm famous since the early 19th century for "decorative objects and furniture in crystal ornamented with bronze." First located at 153 Galerie de Valois, Palais-Royal, and then in 1874 transferred to a corner site at 1 Rue Aubert and 6 Rue Scribe, the business was founded and made prosperous by the widow of Desarnaud-Charpentier. It was shortly after the move to new premises that the Crystal Staircase—a workshop as well as retail outlet—came under the direction of the Frères Pannier, who proceeded to create beautiful vases, most often mounting them on bronze or vermeil. Indeed the mounts became a speciality of the house.

The Musée des Arts Décoratifs has a piece decorated in the style typical of the Pannier brothers (Plates 39, 40). Dating probably from 1888, it is constructed of several strongly colored, differentiated layers, and adorned with a parrot, whose intensely red head stands out from a lunar disk partially obscured by clouds. In dramatic contrast is the jade green of the creature's plumage, revealed in the deepest layers by the cutting wheel.

At the exhibitions of 1892, 1894, and 1898 the Panniers displayed quite a varied production. A generally consistent feature, however, was the use of wheel engraving to enhance the pieces with rather freely drawn themes of insects, parrots, or crows. Supporting the pieces were mounts shaped like waves, rocks, and seaweed.

The Panniers obtained their high-quality colored glass from the Frères Appert and then decorated and mounted the works for sale in their shop. The house signature, usually in diamond point, is "Pannier—Escalier de Cristal."

right: 41. Alphonse Reyen. *Vase with thistles*, c. 1890, height 220 mm/8 3/4″, Musée des Arts Décoratifs, Paris. A talented engraver, Reyen was also a fine and delicate artist, as well as a master of composition, one most often inspired by Japanese art. Signed in diamond point: "Pannier Frères."

below: 42. Alphonse Reyen. (a) *Vase with ears of rye, dragonflies, and other insects*, 1894, height 230 mm/9 1/8″, signed; (b) *Vase with poppies, grasses, and insects*, c. 1900, height 300 mm/11 5/8″. Musée des Arts Décoratifs, Paris. Reyen used intercalary decoration, acid or wheel engraving with equal ease, on forms that are invariably chaste and sober.

The School of Nancy

43. (a) Désiré Christian. *Double-bulb vase decorated with anemones*, c. 1900, height 150 mm/5 7/8"; (b) Désiré Christian. *Cornet vase with orchids*, c. 1900, height 250 mm/9 3/4". Collection A. Lesieutre, Paris. Both signed: "Christian Meisenthal Loth."

"The artistic genius of Lorraine appeared immediately after the 1870 war, like a diamond on a mourning veil." Such were the bold terms that a critic used in 1900 to stress the pioneering role played by the province of Lorraine and its capital city, Nancy, in the rebirth of France's decorative arts.

Lorraine had inherited a tradition of taste, refinement, and virtuoso craftsmanship from the reign of its last sovereign Duke, who was Stanislas (1677–1766), the deposed King of Poland and, more important, the father-in-law of Louis XV. While in Lorraine, Stanislas transformed Nancy into a Rococo glory and the ducal seat at Lunéville into a garden-set palace splendid enough to rival Versailles itself. With the death of Stanislas, his appointment to Lorraine had served its intended purpose, which was to make the province—after more than a thousand years of semi-independence—an integral part of France. So effective was the French policy—and so thoroughly had Stanislas' love of fine things taken hold—that when France lost the Franco-Prussian War in 1870 and ceded the northeastern part of Lorraine to Germany, the disaster simply added new fuel to the burning desire already felt for artistic renewal. Talented Lorrainers fled the occupied areas and, while traveling abroad, gained aesthetic sophistication through exposure to other cultures. Meanwhile, the patriotic feelings of all Lorrainers deepened, which, in turn, motivated the artists among them to excel and to do so by joining the movement toward a purified and revitalized decorative art. From this complex of issues were born a new ethic and a new aesthetic—the School of Nancy (l'Ecole de Nancy).

The galvanizing personality in what would become the School of Nancy was Emile Gallé, a promoter of extraordinary charm and authority about whom gathered Lorraine's painters, sculptors, glassmakers, bookbinders, cabinetmakers, and architects, "each with his own temperament, but sharing the same desire for the rejuvenation of French art" (Gaston Varenne, *Le Pays lorrain*, Feb. 1936). But the thematic thread that bound these artists together was their common interest in nature, which they took as their one abiding source of inspiration, seeking always to capture the supple character of living models and to adapt them to household decoration. "Knowledge of nature is the foundation upon which an artist may support his talent," affirmed Emile Nicolas, a member of the Lorraine group. They also shared a vast enthusiasm for Delacroix, for the Impressionists, and, above all, for Japanese art. The poet of the movement, Emile Gallé, played the same role in France that William Morris or Walter Crane did in England, and his beliefs were comparable to those of John Ruskin, the English aesthetician and critic whose influence fell upon the whole Western world. Did Ruskin not emphasize the preeminently social role of the artist? "It is right that the painter, sculptor, and art worker should be aware of the potential attraction of their works, and become willing educators, apostles of color, line, and beauty. . . ." Thus, by drawing from and integrating the resources of science, art, and industry, the Lorraine artists hoped to find a unity of style strong enough to combat the prejudices of both officialdom and the public. Although latent for a while, their principles became evident after the 1900 Universal Exhibition in Paris, even though, despite the efforts of Gallé, the Lorrainers were not able to show as a group. "The evidence suggests," wrote Gallé, in a call for the establishment of a professional association, "that, given the present world-wide effort to rehabilitate industrial art, there is danger in remaining without ties, a danger of being caught and isolated between the centralized Parisian monopoly and the groups . . . already very well supplied from abroad." And so, when the Lorraine group was formed, by statutes officially lodged in February 1901 under the title of Ecole de Nancy, Alliance Provinciale des Industries d'Art, it clearly marked a desire on the part of Gallé and his colleagues to challenge both Parisian and foreign competition.

Quite naturally, Gallé himself became president of the new society, with the Daum brothers, Louis Majorelle, and Eugène Vallin serving as vice-presidents. The seat of the

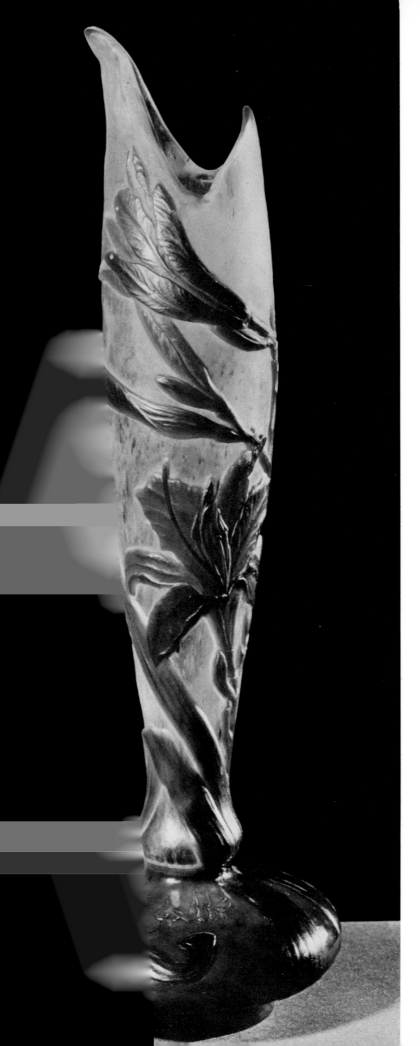

44. Emile Gallé. *Iris Vase,* c. 1900, height 370 mm/14 5/8", collection J.-Cl. Brugnot, Paris. Thanks to deep carving with the wheel, the voluptuously twining flower seems to emerge from the material it embraces, standing out in strong relief against a background dotted with blue-orange metallic-oxide particles.

group was in Nancy, which had remained French. There, in order to establish the local studios upon a firm basis of sound aesthetic and systematic teaching, they gave courses and made plans to found a museum. They also decided to organize some exemplary exhibitions. In this regard their efforts proved very successful at the show mounted in 1903 by the Union Centrale des Arts Décoratifs in the Louvre's Pavillon de Marsan, where the Lorrainers made their debut as a group. In the preface to the catalogue, Emile Gallé pointed out that the aim of his association was to understand natural phenomena and the methods, elements, and character conducive to the creation of a modern ornamental style. Gallé also made the Lorrainers' sources clear: "As naturalists, as decorators, and as industrialists, we have studied the colored garments that clothe all of nature's creatures according to the needs and the milieu in which they exist. For the benefit of our homes, we have deduced from these studies new effects that are at one with the overall harmony of the greater environment."

On the death of Emile Gallé in 1904, his friend Victor Prouvé replaced him as president of the School of Nancy. But despite the loss of its founder, the association remained consistent in its courageous attitudes and continued to promote technical invention and decorative research. In 1908 the society accepted an invitation to exhibit at Strasbourg, in the Palais des Rohan. By then, however, a shift in taste had already set in, and the exhibition became an occasion for lively debate. Henri van de Velde, once a great advocate of Art Nouveau but now an apostle of a more spare, functional, and geometric form of modernism, proclaimed that "every botanical motif carries within itself something trivial." Thus, the whole raison d'être of the School of Nancy—ornamentation inspired by personal sensibility and organic grace—had to give way before what would become a powerful new aesthetic governed by functionalism, rationality, and abstract, mathematical form. From that moment on the School of Nancy suffered progressive decline.

51

ÉMILE GALLÉ

(1846–1904)

In 1844 Charles Gallé, a glassware and ceramics merchant from Clermont-sur-Oise, arrived in Nancy. Over the next thirty years this apparently ordinary event would become the point of departure for the greatest adventure in the history of French glassmaking, from which the name of Emile Gallé, Charles' son, and that of the School of Nancy are inseparable (Plate 44).

Once settled in Nancy, Charles Gallé married a Mademoiselle Reinemer, the daughter of a local mirror-maker of old Protestant stock. On May 4, 1846, their son Emile was born. Meanwhile, Charles Gallé assumed the management of his father-in-law's business, soon adding to it the manufacture of table glass. For this new line he created designs inspired by the flowers of the Lorraine countryside. By 1855 critics could acknowledge in his work "a pleasing originality, a free and curious temperament, and a daring execution." After obtaining forms from the glassworks of Saint-Denis and Pantin, Charles Gallé supervised their decoration at his workshop at Meisenthal. At the same time, he continued to expand the business and in the process took over the faïence works of Saint-Clément, which, following great fame in the 18th century, had fallen into decline. At Saint-Clément, Charles Gallé utilized the antique molds to produce charming pieces in which he could develop his native affinity for an increasingly pronounced naturalism.

Such a family background would seem to have been ideal for nurturing the artistic talent of young Emile Gallé. After serious classical studies at the Lycée Impérial in Nancy, where he inclined towards both philosophy and the natural sciences, the young man, then sixteen years old, chose to follow in the family tradition and began by helping his father. Gifted in design, he made floral compositions as well as devices and emblems for both glass-

ware and faïence. An interest in botany led him to attend the courses of Professor Vaultrin and to go for walks with Dr. Godron, director of Nancy's Botanical Gardens (founded under Duke Stanislas) and author of *La Flore Française* and *La Flore Lorraine*. Emile also became friendly with Antoine Zeiller, a famous paleobotanist and the Lorraine's official Engineer of Bridges and Roads. What time he had left Emile spent botanizing, at first near Pompey, where the flora of Lorraine are particularly rich, and then in the forest of Haye, in the Vosges, in the Savoy Alps, in Alsace, and even as far away as Switzerland and northern Italy. He rediscovered the emotions first felt by those great 18th-century Romantics, Bernardin de Saint-Pierre and Jean-Jacques Rousseau. The result was a splendid section in *Ecrits pour l'Art,** where Gallé the poet proves himself a true botanist. Meanwhile, this prodigy also took lessons in drawing from Professor Casse and in plein-air landscape painting from the artist Paul Pierre.

On the advice of his father, Gallé traveled in Germany from 1862 to 1864, "to see and understand." At the important German cultural center of Weimar, he had his first lesson in modeling and advanced science. There he met the celebrated pianist-composer Franz Liszt, who played for him the works of his son-in-law, Richard Wagner. Already a convinced Wagnerian, Gallé would remain one all his life.

In 1864 Gallé became the designer in the family business, and to familiarize himself with the smallest details of faïence and glass, he decided in 1866 to go to Meisenthal in the valley of the Sarre, there to work with the firm of Burgun, Schwerer & Cie. It was this enterprise, which still

*An anthology of Gallé's own writings, published in 1908 with an introduction by Mme Gallé.

exists, that provided the senior Gallé with glass blanks, and by entering into the operation, Emile Gallé hoped "to learn the trade" and, above all, to learn the chemistry of glass.

A trip to England enabled Gallé to admire the decorative masterpieces in the Brandt collection, as well as those in the South Kensington Museums (now the Victoria & Albert Museum). The young man also saw the famous *Portland Vase* (an amphora of cobalt blue dating from the 1st century B.C. in the British Museum), along with all the other antiquities and the Oriental collections.

In 1870, Gallé had hardly returned to his father at Saint-Clément when war broke out between France and Germany. Gallé immediately volunteered and did service in the 23rd Line Regiment. Brutal but brief, the conflict left France stripped of Alsace and the northeastern sector of Lorraine.

With peace restored in 1871, Gallé again traveled to London, this time to represent his father at the "Arts of France" exhibition. On his way back, he stopped in Paris, where the Cluny Museum and, above all, the Louvre held his attention. It took him several months to satisfy his eager curiosity, and to study ancient techniques.

Meisenthal and Saint-Clément were both in territory now annexed by Germany, which made them difficult of access to the Gallés. For a while, therefore, the younger man took work at the faïence factory of Raon-l'Etape. Meanwhile, in 1873, he moved into *La Garenne* ("The Rabbit Warren"), the great Neoclassical house with extensive gardens that his father built in Nancy at 39 Avenue de la Garenne. In 1874 the senior Gallé retired and turned the business over to his son, who forthwith set about to regroup the firm's various activities—personnel and equipment for faïence and glass manufacture, research, design, composition, decoration, and engraving (Plate 46)—in Nancy, there creating the embryo of future factories. Then, with his marriage in 1875 to Henriette Grimm, Emile Gallé was permanently settled in Nancy.

A compulsive worker, Gallé increased the business considerably. In 1883 he had to build new, large workshops, not only for faïence and glass but also for cabinetmaking. He kept a room at the center of the complex, where he worked on his projects, confiding the execution, at least partially, to his collaborators. The Gallé firm now employed a great many artists and craftsmen, and by 1889 the staff numbered about three hundred. The director himself taught the decorators and continued to organize new design studios, where "many living models were available, thanks to the garden . . . and to the collections of natural history." Gallé sent his own watercolors, executed from nature, to his studio heads. Moreover, he forbade

46. Emile Gallé. *Bowl with insects, butterflies, and flowers.* c. 1875–80, height 150 mm/5 7/8″, collection J. Lorch, Paris. Working with his father, who had taken over the Saint-Clément faïence works, Gallé found his first themes in faïence, where butterflies and other insects fly about among the flowers.

his collaborators to produce a single flower without having the model before their eyes, but allowed them every liberty in interpretation. "It is necessary to have a pronounced bias in favor of motifs taken from flora and fauna, while giving them a free expression," he said in 1889. It was about this time, and up to 1896, that some exchange of correspondence suggests a secret arrangement between Emile Gallé and Burgun, Schwerer & Cie, by which the Meisenthal company would undertake to produce glass according to the precise directions and over the signature of Emile Gallé. But the official document of this agreement has been lost, which leaves some question about the precise degree of Burgun, Schwerer's involvement in the production of Gallé glass. It is thought that Gallé committed himself to giving the firm regular work, but on the express condition that his methods be kept secret. It would seem that this activity was to be supervised by Désiré Christian, which creates some confusion, since the connection between Gallé and Christian is indisputable, and the similarity of the techniques and themes employed by the two masters can make their work extremely difficult to distinguish (Plate 43).

Emile Gallé opened several shops: In 1885 at 12 Rue Richer in Paris; in 1897 at Frankfurt-am-Main; then in London. He exhibited his works regularly, and his contributions were always eagerly awaited. In 1878 he participated for the first time in a Universal Exhibition, occupying a whole pavilion 30 meters long. In the course of an extraordinary career Gallé received four Gold Medals and progressively gained world-wide fame, mainly through the agency of the big international exhibitions:

1884: "Stone, Wood, Earth, Glass" show in Paris. Gallé won a Gold Medal.
1893: Universal Exhibition in Chicago.
1894: Exposition d'Art Décoratif in Nancy.
1897: Munich Exhibition, where Gallé was responsible for the triumph of French decorative arts and himself won a medal.
1900: Universal Exhibition in Paris, which marked the crowning moment in Gallé's career. It brought him two Grands Prix, another Gold Medal, and the status of commander in the Legion of Honor. His works were displayed in a somewhat theatrical arrangement, including a reconstructed glass furnace on the front of which was inscribed a verse from Hesiod:

Since men are forgers and prevaricators
Give me the evil demons of the Fire!
So that all men may learn to practice
Justice!

1901: International Exhibition in Dresden.
1902: Exhibition of Decorative Arts in Turin.

Covered with glory and honors, Gallé became a founding member of the Société des Beaux-Arts in Paris, as well as a member of several learned societies. On May 17, 1900, he was admitted to Nancy's prestigious Académie Stanislas. His acceptance speech, a remarkable statement on Symbolist decoration, is basic to an understanding of the Gallé aesthetic. In 1901, he founded the School of Nancy and became its president, with Antonin Daum, Louis Majorelle, and Eugène Vallin serving as vice-presidents.

A man of deep social conscience, Gallé joined with Victor Prouvé (Plate 45) to take part in the establishment of the Université Populaire, also in the launching of a journal called *L'Etoile de l'Est* ("The Star of the East"), which he helped to underwrite.

Gallé enjoyed the support of several major patrons, among them Germain Bapst, Edmond Taigny, Léon Clairy, Henri Hirsch, and Baron de Rothschild. Museums also acquired his works. Some of Gallé's unique pieces were made on special order for commemorative purposes; others to express the author's gratitude and admiration for people in the worlds of science and the arts, or to pay homage to crowned heads.

Gallé even received the tribute of being widely copied. "Imitations in the Gallé style have been made," he wrote, "and I am pleased. May moderation, sobriety, and good taste always preside over the use made of my small discoveries." This, unfortunately, was not always the case. Most often, indeed, Gallé's imitators lost the spirit and meaning of the model and kept only the purely decorative aspect.

In 1904 newspapers reported that Gallé's health had been "underminded by a mysterious illness, probably provoked by an intensive hemorrhage." In reality he suffered leukemia and died on September 23, 1904. His son-in-law, Professor Perdrizet, head of the Faculté des Lettres at Nancy University, succeeded Gallé as director of the firm and remained in that post until the cessation of activity in 1931. Sadly, the factory had failed to maintain the lively creativity promoted by Emile Gallé. Instead, it relied on existing models and did so without imagination or artistic invention.

47. Conceived by Gallé and executed by Eugène Vallin for one of the studios at *La Garenne* in Nancy, these oaken portals bear an inscription whose words constitute the profession of faith that informed the whole of Emile Gallé's work: *Nos racines sont au fond des bois, au bord des sources, sur les mousses* ("Our roots are in the depths of the woods, on the banks of springs, among mosses"). Musée de l'Ecole de Nancy.

The only object surviving today from Emile Gallé's own studios is a door that the master conceived and had made by Eugène Vallin (Plate 47). Preserved in the garden of the Musée de l'Ecole de Nancy, it carries this couplet: "Our roots are in the depths of the woods, on the banks of the springs, among mosses." Here was his true profession of faith, Gallé tells us in *Ecrits pour l'Art*, giving as his source of inspiration *La Circulation de Paris—1866* by Jacobus Moleschott, who, perhaps, influenced by Baudelaire, wrote: "It is through plants that we have our attachment to the earth; they are our roots."

left: 48. Emile Gallé. *Translucent bowl imitating coral, shaded in black and ornamented with four Roman emperor portrait medallions,* c. 1880, height 70 mm/ 2 3/4″, Musée des Arts Décoratifs, Paris. Here Gallé has taken his inspiration from the ancient glyptic art of cameo carving.

right: 49. Emile Gallé. *Vase with silver mount, styled in the 18th-century manner,* height 150 mm/5 7/8″, private collection.

GALLÉ'S SOURCES OF INSPIRATION

Emile Gallé was the product of an epoch torn between strong ties to the past and an equally strong desire for renewal. Given the circumstances in which he found himself—"without an education capable of facilitating the start of my career, without a master in the art of adapting flora and fauna to the exigencies of various materials and processes, with no continuing tradition, no overall view"—Gallé had to draw on all possible sources. This is why his work reflected numerous influences, before the artist found the means to express his own innermost feelings.

In his native town, Nancy, Gallé could, of course, learn about antique styles and the known practices in decorative glass (Plate 48). Taking what he could from these resources, he decorated glass pieces with genre scenes styled after the 18th century, with 17th-century Dutch landscapes, or in the manner of Venetian and Bohemian glass (Plates 49–51). But even here, some personal details identify the works as interpretations rather than slavish imitations. Gallé attempted, even at this early date, to make his glass iridescent, like that found in Gallo-Roman excavations, many examples of which were in the Musée de Nancy. Then there was the town itself, which still had its exquisite 18th-century appearance, and Gallé cannot have been indifferent to the riches inherited from the reign of Duke Stanislas. Thus, it must be more than mere coincidence that Gallé's interlace patterns recall the ironwork of Jean Lamour, the master craftsman who created the splendid wrought-iron grillework that contributes so much to the incredible beauty of Nancy's Place Stanislas, built in 1752–56 by the architect Emmanuel Héré. But in his father's studio Gallé found another tradition, that of faïences with "lifelike" decorations, in which butterflies

flutter about in the midst of bouquets of field flowers. The source suggested here lay in "that flora of Lorraine, the ancient yet forever-young inspiration of his vases . . . executed with freshness and innocence." It was no great distance from the decoration of faïence to that of glass, and Gallé quickly made the move from one to the other (Plates 46–52). As early as 1867 he received comment for the drawings he prepared for his father's workshop. One critic, a friend of Roger Marx, even said: "Emile has a great deal of taste; he is an artist; and, furthermore, he knows botany . . . He cannot fail to effect the revolution he is equipped to undertake." That moment had not yet come, and it would arrive only after a long germination.

During his stay in Paris Gallé, of course, discovered artistic resources unknown in Nancy. In the Egyptian rooms of the Louvre he was enthralled by the hieratic order of the bas-reliefs and by the stylized naturalism of the lotus flowers and beetles. He liked the expressive simplification of the gestures and attitudes, and felt himself in intellectual accord with the restrained sobriety of Egyptian art. In this collection he also saw the oldest known pâtes-de-verre. Several of Gallé's pieces testify to his entry into this antique world, and, writing in 1884, he advises us to see in them "mystical beetles, Egyptian harvesters, sphinxes, and lotus flowers." Finally, however, these models proved too limiting and rigid for the rapidly developing Gallé.

With Greco-Roman antiquity Gallé could feel more at home. His classical studies had taught what he characterized as "that ancient secular system, the theory of the beautiful, jealously maintained since Plato." It tempted him for a while, and he made some beautiful vases, in which he adapted to his own romantic sensibility the eternal theme

50. Emile Gallé. *Transparent vase, ornamented with a fishing scene*, c. 1878, height 130 mm/5 1/8″, collection G. Courtois, Paris. A charmingly simple scene painted in gray grisaille, framed with red and gold shellwork modeled after 18th-century faïences.

below left: 51. Emile Gallé. *Cup decorated with a stag-hunt scene in brown grisaille and footed in transparent glass*, c. 1878, height 125 mm/4 7/8″, collection J.-Cl. Brugnot, Paris. 18th-century Bohemian glassware provided both subject and style.

below right: 52. Emile Gallé. *Vase decorated with a grisaille fishing scene, surrounded by an enameled sheaf of field flowers*, c. 1878, height 151 mm/ 5 7/8″, collection J. Lorch, Paris. Love for the field flowers of his native Lorraine motivated Gallé to become a botanist while still a boy; it then constituted his primary source of inspiration throughout a long artistic career.

left: **53.** Emile Gallé. *Goblet enameled with ornamental foliage and arabesques,* c. 1880, height 100 mm/3 7/8", Kunstmuseum, Coll. Hentrich, Düsseldorf.

below: **54.** Emile Gallé. *Confection dish, imitating rock crystal, enameled with ornamental foliage,* c. 1878–84, height 130 mm/5 1/8", collection J. Lorch, Paris.

of Orpheus and Euridyce—love's triumph over death (Fig. 96).* But classical rigor could not fully satisfy Gallé's passionate nature; thus, his figures embody less the canon of Polykleitos than the artificial languor of the late 19th-century "painters of the soul." Greek antiquity offered guides to form, if not to content, and throughout Gallé's work one can find, among new or even "baroque" shapes, certain pure forms borrowed from the antique repertory, such as amphora, craters, and aryballos (Plate 138).

The Galerie d'Apollon in the Louvre, with its fantastic crystal, cut glassware, and priceless Renaissance gems, proved a revelation for Gallé. Fascinated, he was tempted to follow Eugène Rousseau in imitating such density of material: "Do not glassmakers have the power to shape agates, marbles, rock crystals?" In memory of his visit to the Apollo Gallery, Gallé, calling himself "a counterfeiting stonecutter," imitated rock crystal for the *Coupe des Quatre-Saisons,* the decoration of which was inspired by Raphael's Vatican Loggia. It appeared in the 1878 Universal Exhibition, along with a sweetmeat dish in Renaissance shape. Something of the type can be seen in Plate 54.

It was in Paris too that Gallé encountered the methods of Eugène Rousseau, his "tricks of the trade," his overlay or cased glass, his agate and crackled glass (Plates 26, 27). They provided him with another experimental springboard towards new researches in material offering chunky thickness and special effects (Plates 55, 58). In addition to

*Louis de Fourcaud indicated in 1903 that there were other Gallé vases with mythological themes: *Medici, Apollo, Bacchanale,* now lost. Sensitive to the currents of his time, Gallé seems to have been more at ease with freer symbolic interpretations, such as *La Nuit* ("Night"), *Le Silence* ("Silence"), *Le Sommeil* ("Sleep"), or *La Fortune Endormie* ("Sleeping Fortune"), now in the Musée des Arts Décoratifs.

left: 55. Emile Gallé. *Cigar box*, c. 1884, height 80 mm/3 1/8″, Kunst-museum, Coll. Hentrich, Düsseldorf. Gallé himself described this box in an exhibition note: "Cigar box ornamented with a cameo represent-ing a grasshopper in flight, cut in solid clear crystal, in which the light emerald marbling simulates the green stripes of the rosy enameled wings. The remainder of the vase shows Egyptian harvesters engraved in gold."

right: 56. Emile Gallé. *Vase with enameled interlacing and intaglio-en-graved spirals*, c. 1880, height 70 mm/2 3/4″, collection J.-Cl. Brugnot, Paris. Much influenced by Islamic art, the design of this vase depends upon a harmonious combination of deep cutting and enamel.

below: 57. Emile Gallé. *Covered enameled vase showing on one side the Duke of Burgundy and on the other the Archbishop of Rheims*, c. 1884, height 250 mm/9 3/4″, collection F. Marcilhac, Paris. Gallé here submitted to the current rage for everything medieval, going so far as to engrave the inscriptions in Old French.

the simulation of gemstones, Gallé owed to Rousseau, above all else, one absolutely determining discovery—the possibility of adapting to European art glass certain of the shapes and decorations traditional to China and Japan.

Always seeking new interest, Gallé found the Middle Ages, led there by those great medievalists, Viollet-le-Duc, Jules Michelet, and Victor Hugo. Gallé responded to the age's fascination with everything feudal and created an ar-morial or heraldic style that bore the stamp of his own per-sonal romanticism. The phase brought forth *Ballade des Dames du Temps Jadis,* inspired by François Villon (Plate 92), in addition to a series of Lorraine archbishops and an evocation of Joan of Arc (Plate 57). In the same period, around 1884, he also fashioned a group of tankards dec-orated with popular themes (Plate 62), and later contin-ued to make them as the public demanded.

In the brilliant fantasies of 13th–14th-century Islamic art, with its arabesques and flat, ornamental foliage, Gallé perceived color to be a new means of achieving beauty and elegance. Not only had the excavations at Dams, Rages, and El Racka uncovered ceramics and glass decorated with astonishing enamels, but, moreover, Joseph Brocard had just launched the fashion for mosque lamps enameled in the Arab manner (Plate 16). After meeting Brocard at the 1884 Palais de l'Industrie exhibition, Gallé was tempted to follow the new mode as it was then established. But instead, he rediscovered for himself and indeed even surpassed the favorite Arab method of applying hard enamels to glass (Plates 53, 56). On some pieces Kufic in-scriptions testify to Gallé's source of inspiration. But to the French master, the Islamicized pieces were, more than anything else, an exercise in style—soon abandoned, or

used only occasionally, once he had exhausted its possibilities for him and his clientele. What remained permanently with Gallé were a new, Oriental sense of color harmony and of flat, decorative pattern—and, of course, the technique of hard, highly finished enamel (Plate 59).

Such was Gallé's creative fervor that the imitation of antique prototypes, themselves often mere copies, could not prove satisfying for long. But in contemporary Impressionist painting he at last found the expression of a sensibility sympathetic to his own, "beginning in that warm contact with nature so necessary to the artist." The exhibition organized by the Impressionists in 1874, at Nadar's photography studio on the Rue des Capucines, constituted a genuine pictorial revolution. Light invaded their canvases according to the subtle variations of hour or season, and played over those most mobile of nature's elements—air and water. Like the new painters, Gallé tried to translate his "impressions" through the direct study of flora and fauna. In tonalities that were sometimes light and sometimes somber, but most often in complementary contrasts, he created a mood (Plates 60, 61). And as the Impressionists matured into a new sensibility, he shared their belief that, before everything else, art must express the personal feeling of its creator, his vision of the world, whether real or imaginary. Realized in blurred, evanescent outlines, seemingly dissolved in a halo of light, some of the glassmaker's decorations helped open the way to abstraction. Sometimes Gallé even managed to capture the luminous insubstantiality of atmosphere (Plates 63, 64).

In the same period, and like every other advanced artist in France, Gallé made the momentous discovery of Japa-

right: 60. Emile Gallé. *Flask engraved and enameled with thistles and small flowers*, c. 1890, height 135 mm/ 5 1/4", collection J.-Cl. Brugnot, Paris.

far right: 61. Emile Gallé. *Vase with orchids*, c. 1895–1900, height 252 mm/9 7/8", collection J.-Cl. Brugnot, Paris.

below left: 62. Emile Gallé. *Enameled tankard decorated with a figure*, c. 1884, height 100 mm/3 7/8", collection J. Lorch, Paris. On a form modeled after 18th-century German glass, Gallé has amused himself by representing a M. Dumollet, hero of a popular song.

below right: 63. Emile Gallé. *Cornet vase decorated with plants and butterflies*, c. 1900, height 220 mm/ 8 5/8", collection J.-Cl. Brugnot, Paris. Influenced by the Impressionists, Gallé makes his evanescent design of febrile vegetation and insects vibrate with a thousand delicate, luminous touches.

left: 64. Emile Gallé. *Les Rochers dans la mer* ("Rocks in the Sea"), c. 1900, height 550 mm/21 1/2", collection J.-Cl. Brugnot, Paris. This bronze-mounted vase creates a whole ambience of exotic revery. Like a painter playing with colors and values, Gallé opens our imaginations to infinite horizons.

below: 65. Emile Gallé. *Autumn Crocuses*, c. 1900, height 300 mm/11 3/4", Kunstmuseum, Coll. Hentrich, Düsseldorf. Gallé saw a melancholy beauty in the *veilleuses d'automne* (fall field crocuses called "autumn lights"), which he made the theme of a whole series of fine vases with shapes harmoniously allied to the décor.

left: 66. Hiroshige. *Japanese print*, private collection. The influence of Hiroshige, together with that of Utamaro, could be felt throughout European art in the second half of the 19th century.

right: 67. Emile Gallé. *Columbine Vase*, c. 1898, height 230 mm/9 1/8″, private collection. In this vase, mounted on gilded bronze cast in a naturalistic style, the composition, the tonal gradations, the color contrasts, and the supple lines all attest to Gallé's thorough assimilation of the lessons taught by Japanese art.

below left: 68. Emile Gallé. *Vase with flowers and bats*, c. 1892, height 260 mm/10 1/4″, private collection. The theme of the bat, a favorite of the Symbolists, represents a tribute paid by Gallé to his mentor Robert de Montesquiou, who had recently published *Les Chauves-Souris* ("The Bats"), a collection of poems. Two of the poet's lines are inscribed on the vase: *La bonté de la nuit caresse l'âme sombre/Le silence des nuits panse l'âme blessée* ("The kindness of the night caresses the dark soul/The silence of the nights binds the wounded spirit").

below right: 69. Emile Gallé. *Vase with autumn leaves*, c. 1900, height 150 mm/5 7/8″, private collection. Opaque glass and a grisaille ground create an autumnal, melancholy mood. Dead leaves float about, those *feuilles des douleurs passées* ("leaves of past sorrows") so dear to Maurice Maeterlinck.

left: 70. Emile Gallé. *Vase with iris*, c. 1900, height 250 mm/9 3/4″, collection A. Lesieutre, Paris. Engraved with lines from Maeterlinck: *Toutes les âmes sont prêtes/Il faut cependant que l'une d'elle commence./Pourquoi ne pas être celle qui commence?* ("All souls are ready/One of them, however, must take the first step./Why not be the one to begin?"). Like many of France's *fin-de-siècle* artists, Gallé was much drawn to the Symbolist poetry of Maeterlinck, especially to the mysticism that lay at the heart of the Belgian master's thought.

right: 71. Emile Gallé. *Chimera Vase*, c. 1878, height 100 mm/3 7/8″, Kunstmuseum, Coll. Hentrich, Düsseldorf. The chimera with its staring eyes and menacing air is China's mythical and symbolic counterpart of the lion. Gallé combines the motif with that of grasshoppers and flowers. True to the spirit of the piece is the signature, rendered as a Chinese ideogram.

nese art, recently introduced to Europe in the form of colored wood-block prints by Hiroshige and Utamaro (Plate 66). These artists expressed themselves in a free, asymmetrical manner, thanks to their intimate knowledge of nature and to the power of their supple line. With flat, highly contrasted colors and collapsed spaces, the Japanese artists created not a literal setting but rather a suggestive one, thereby evoking images of great poetry and feeling. Gallé understood the essence of this eminently symbolist art, in which he saw reflected the enduring presence of God. Discussions with his Japanese friend Takasima must have been helpful. Even so, it was at an early date that the Frenchman had an inkling of the Orient's harmonious sensibility. Certainly he would have seen the Eastern art at the 1867 Universal Exhibition, especially the stoneware of the tea ceremony. Indeed, it enchanted him. Still, the influence of Japan did not appear in Gallé's work until 1878, and then only tentatively. A critic noted "some works soberly decorated, with blades of grass rendered in the Japanese manner." Finally, around 1884, Gallé let nature overrun his vases and thus gave free rein to his most important source of inspiration (Plates 65, 67, 75). Like the Japanese, he responded to the symbolic charge emanating from nature; thus, the humble poppies of the field, once transformed by his imagination and artistry, became funerary urns "whose very purpose induces a sense of calm, peace, and rest" (Plate 99).

The "correspondences" felt by Gallé recall Charles Baudelaire's pioneering search for the "language of flowers and mute things" (Plate 76). Gallé refers to Baudelaire many times, and both the poet and the glassmaker possessed the same acuteness of vision, as well as the same refined sentiment towards things both animate and inanimate. Like visionaries, they sought beyond appearances for "the character and feeling contained within." For Gallé the time was ripe, possibly made ready long before by his reading in Sylvestre de Sacy's Bible, in *Thousand and One Nights*, or in the *Tales* of Hoffmann, all perfect for endowing the adolescent with a taste for symbol and fantasy (Plate 71).* Gallé also discovered Jean-Jacques Grandville, the "delicious symbolist" and illustrator of the first half of the 19th century, and learned "to read in his animated flowers and stars" strange symbolic and even quasi-surrealist mutations. The important lecture given by Gallé on May 17, 1900, which marked his admission to the Académie Stanislas, provides a good summary of his Baudelairian aesthetic of "symbolist decoration." "Poets, masters of words, are also masters of decoration; they have a genius for the image; they create the symbol." "Baudelaire," he continued, "has made a grand formulation of his idea of harmonious resonances in the immensity of creation:

La Nature est un temple où de vivants piliers
Laissent parfois sortir de confuses paroles.
L'homme y passe à travers des forêts de symboles
Qui l'observent avec des regards familiers."

(Nature is a temple where living pillars
Sometimes allow confused words to escape.
Man passes there through forests of symbols
That watch him with familiar glances.)

*All suggested by Charles de Meixmoron de Dombasle, president of the Académie Stanislas, in his reply to Gallé's admission lecture of 1900.

72. Emile Gallé. *Le Figuier* ("The Fig Tree"), c. 1900, height 580 mm/ 22 3/4″, Musée de l'Ecole de Nancy. This vase has been engraved with lines from Victor Hugo: *Car tous les hommes sont les fils d'un même Père,/Ils sont la même larme et sortent du même oeil* ("Since all men are the sons of the same Father,/They are the same tear and come from the same eye"). Gallé joins the poet to celebrate the fraternity of men, all the while lamenting their sad, precarious condition: *laissant rouler des pleurs humains le long de ce calice* ("letting human tears run down the length of this chalice").

The connections between these two artists are almost endless, and many of Gallé's vases carry quotations from Baudelaire. One of the craftsman's wood marquetry works is called *Les Fleurs du Mal,** and among the glass Gallé exhibited at the Salon du Champs de Mars in 1892, one has the title of *Sur un Thème de Baudelaire* ("On a Theme from Baudelaire"). To such a degree was Gallé influenced by the poet that, unconsciously or not, he adopted most of his mentor's enthusiasms, especially as these were articulated in *Curiosités esthétiques*, published in 1860 and reissued in 1879. They included Richard Wagner, the great German Romantic composer whose operas express the grandeur of nature and the solemnity of human passions. With *Parsifal* in mind, Gallé planned in 1894 to make a glass Holy Grail, complete with tabernacle. He also shared with Baudelaire an admiration for the sincere and soulful Marceline Desbordes-Valmore, believing with her that "blessed be the somber corners where our hearts are alone." But above all others there was Victor Hugo, in whom both Baudelaire and Gallé recognized "the translator and decipherer of symbols, chosen to express the mystery of life through poetry." For the intellectual in Gallé, Victor Hugo was the great man, admirable not only in his liberal and generous ideas, but in his courage as well. In 1862, when *Les Misérables* appeared, Gallé was sixteen, and it is easy to understand how this social epic, the most popular of its time in France, could leave an indelible mark upon a young and sensitive nature. Later, but still faithful to Victor Hugo, Gallé would often draw

*T. Charpentier, "L'Art de Gallé a-t-il été influencé par Baudelaire?" *Gazette des Beaux-Arts* (May–June 1963).

far left: 73. Emile Gallé. *Le Sense de la Vie* ("The Meaning of Life"), c. 1889, height 145 mm/5 5/8″, collection J.-Cl. Brugnot, Paris. Nasturtium-decorated and engraved with lines from Victor Hugo: *Je n'ai rien d'autre à faire ici-bas que d'aimer* ("I have no task here below other than to love"). The vase is furthermore dedicated by Gallé to Edmond Rostand.

left: 74. Emile Gallé. *Vase decorated with enamel flowers and arabesques and, in reserve, a knight,* c. 1884–89, height 280 mm/11″, collection J. Lorch, Paris. Like Victor Hugo, who had such a strong influence on him, Gallé sent forth his knight to defend his social ideals of justice and truth. "My career is Justice," he said.

below left: 75. Emile Gallé. *Vase painted and enameled with plants and birds,* c. 1878–84, height 320 mm/12 1/5″, collection S. Deschamps, Paris. Here Gallé captured all the poetry of Japanese art, in a landscape composed of flora and exotic fauna.

below right: 76. Emile Gallé. *Le Coudrier* ("The Hazel Tree"), 1895, height 220 mm/8 5/8″, private collection. *Non de perles brodé mais de toutes mes larmes* ("Embroidered, not with pearls, but with all my tears"). This engraved line from Baudelaire seems to affirm that Gallé and the poet looked at the universe with the same keen eye, and followed the same Symbolist quest through *le langage des fleurs et des choses muettes* ("the language of flowers and silent things"). With such poetry as his guide, Gallé made the glass ewer evoke at once both the frosts of winter and the first fruits of spring.

below: 77. Emile Gallé. *Vase with floral decoration*, c. 1900–04, height 350 mm/13 3/4″, private collection.

right 78. Emile Gallé. *Vase with floral decoration*, c. 1900–04, height 240 mm/9 3/8″, private collection.

right center: 79. Emile Gallé. *Vase with floral decoration*, c. 1900–04, height 370 mm/14 1/2″, private collection.

far right: 80. Emile Gallé. *Vase with floral decoration*, c. 1900–04, height 320 mm/12 1/2″, private collection.

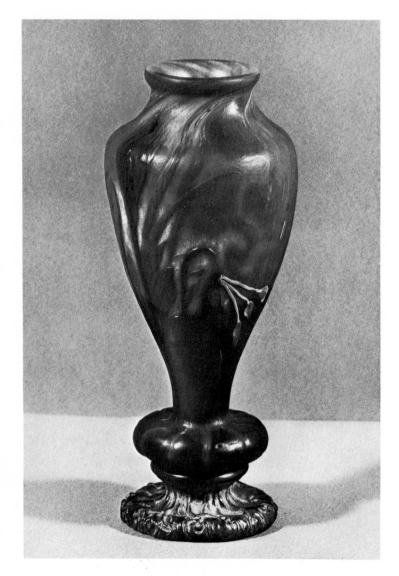

on the great writer's major ideas about justice, peace, love, liberty, and truth (Plates 73, 74). Like Hugo, he believed in the importance of the artist's role in society, for "how can one express life, if one does not take part in it wholeheartedly?" When Gallé wrote "My career is Justice," he seemed to make himself the spokesman for Victor Hugo, as when also he wrote on the vase entitled *Le Figuier* (Plate 72): "Since all men are the sons of the same Father, /They are the same tear and come from the same eye."

To a lesser degree, other thinkers, poets, and writers also moved Gallé. It is impossible to cite them all, but the numerous literary references with which Gallé sprinkled his writings reflect his great learning, which he put at the service of artistic expression. Certain names, however, recur more frequently than others, such as the aristocrat and poet Robert de Montesquiou, from whom he borrowed, among others, the theme of the bat—a favorite animal of the Symbolists (Plate 68). In Maurice Maeterlinck, the Belgian Symbolist poet, Gallé found the melancholy verses to inspire several vases (Plate 69): "When the leaves fall one by one on the reflection of the firmament in the water of dream and mist." The poet's "leaves of past sorrows" offer a link between Symbolism and an attitude bordering on mysticism (Plate 70): "All souls are ready/ One of them, however, must take the first step./ Why not be the one to begin?" The refined Sully Prudhomme, whose *Réflexions* (made "to calm humanity") appeared in 1892, appealed to Gallé because of his ideas on justice and happiness.

Furthermore, Gallé never renounced the Romantics of his youth: Lamartine, Chateaubriand, and Musset. Like them, he loved to give free rein to his imagination and dreams (Plate 95). But in the end, whatever other source

The vases on these two pages illustrate the continuity of the floral theme in Gallé's art. After representing the motif in a naturalistic manner throughout its various stages of growth and development, Gallé gradually decomposed and schematized the image until he had taken it to the brink of pure abstraction. While the stem became the principal decorative element, the shape of the vase, with its bulb base, followed the same stylistic evolution as the theme.

right: 81. Emile Gallé. *Vase with floral decoration*, c. 1900–04, height 320 mm/12 1/2″, private collection.

he may have drawn upon, Gallé always turned back to his one most transcendent inspiration—nature. In 1884, at the time of the Universal Exhibition, he summed up his work as follows: "The jury will surely note that nature is always my point of departure, but that I try to liberate myself from it in time to achieve a personal character and accent." This capacity for nature—this passion even—went back to Gallé's youth. We know with what enthusiasm he studied botany, first in Lorraine, then in the Alps, and how he wandered through the countryside, not only as an artist, but also as a true botanist. Everywhere he sought to adapt nature, for in nature he saw the reflection "of his individuality and thoughts, his concern for logic, his emotion, imagination, enthusiasm, and sincerity—since it is life." Gallé even called one vase *Communion with Nature*, and in 1901 he confirmed his debt to the biological world: "The love of flowers reigned in my family; it was an inherited passion, a salvation. I cultivated what was a paternal tradition." This passion became an intellectual and emotional cult, prompting him sometimes to copy naturalistic forms in varying ways, or to decompose natural forms into their organic parts—or, again, to schematize them to the point of abstraction (Plates 77–81).

His best collaborators were the horticulturists of Nancy—Victor Lemoine and his son, and the gardener Schultz—all creators of rare orchids, begonias, and primulas. In 1884, out of gratitude to Lemoine, who had developed a variety of primula in honor of Madame Gallé, the glassmaker fashioned a vase inspired by a verse from Dante. In the garden around his house, he cultivated exotic plants side by side with the native Lorraine species (Plate 85). All the passionate terms, the controlled lyri-

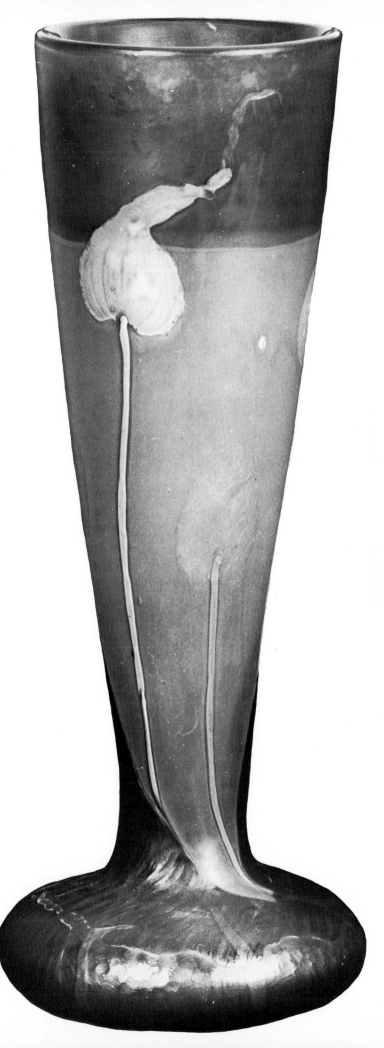

82. Emile Gallé. *La Soude* ("Soda"), height 460 mm/18″, Musée de l'Ecole de Nancy. Made for the Belgian chemist Ernest Solvay, this vase seems to metamorphose before our eyes—at first raw crystal in the matrix, and then matter in fusion—thanks to human genius and industry.

right: 83. Emile Gallé. *Jellyfish Cup*, c. 1895–1900, height 300 mm/11 7/8″, collection J.-Cl. Brugnot, Paris. While oceanography remained a new science, Gallé used the flight of a disheveled jellyfish to capture all the fascinating and unexpected mystery of the underwater world.

cism, and the botanical erudition with which Gallé wrote about "floriculture" are fully evident in *Ecrits pour l'Art* (1908), a collection of the master's "notices" on glass.

But for Gallé, nature is never still. He makes us hear the murmuring of the trees in the woods, the chirping of the cicadas (Plate 84), or the ripple of living water welling up from forest springs. A breath of fresh breeze passes by. But nature is also the vehicle of messages, and a definition offered by Louis de Fourcaud accords perfectly with Gallé's glass: "Art must be the concrete devotion that man pays to his abstract ideas in the presence and with the help of nature." Gallé liked to quote his favorite authorities, doing so "in order to edify the collectors," but also because "the French spirit loves clarity."

No statement about Gallé would be complete without mention of the great role that certain scientific discoveries played in his art and thought. Like all his contemporaries, this constantly evolving and continuously inquiring man was struck by the enormous scientific progress that had been made by the end of the century. Science offered the decorative artist "virgin symbols unknown to our ancestors, yet perfect for opening eyes long closed to familiar things." In 1870–75 geological societies were organized and important treatises published, providing what seemed to be satisfactory answers to the old, old question of how the terrestrial globe had been formed. The vases *Géologie* of 1906 and *La Soude* ("Soda") of 1902 celebrate the riches of the soil and their exploitation by man (Plate 82). Then there was the still inarticulate science of oceanography, which offered new possibilities for underwater exploration. The mysterious, mythical world imagined by Victor Hugo in his *Travailleurs de la Mer* ("Toilers of the Sea") had

left: 84. Emile Gallé. *Cicada Cup*, c. 1900, height 200 mm/7 7/8", collection J.-Cl. Brugnot, Paris. Nature, as described by Gallé, is in perpetual movement; thus, the cicadas fly in the midst of twigs and pine cones. The vase seems hot with summer and filled with the rhythm of steady stridulation.

below left: 85. Emile Gallé. *Vase with ears of grain*, c. 1900, height 220 mm/8 5/8", collection J.-Cl. Brugnot, Paris. "Who prevents us from taking cereals and their flowers as themes?" asked Gallé in *Ecrits pour l'Art.*

below right: 86. Emile Gallé. *Vase with shellfish, mollusks, seaweed, and starfish*, c. 1895–1900, collection Manoukian, Paris. This piece again illustrates the lively interest Gallé had in the aquatic world, which gave him so many original designs, often lending themselves to numerous variations on the same theme.

become a reality. Always lyrical in his work, Gallé would now achieve true poetry. "The crystalline jellyfish, among other creatures," he wrote, "can breathe nuances and unexpected curves into the glass calyxes" (Plate 83). Everything that climbs, crawls, or glides in the depths of the sea—crustaceans, molluscs, fish among marine "floriculture"—Gallé never ceased describing them in dreamlike works (Plate 86). This strange world excited his imagination. The taste may be compared to his love of the unusual, as when "in the process of conceiving a decoration, wraithlike phantoms—symbols of empiricism and of the denial of causality—begin to appear. . . ." The occasion for these comments was the *Vase Pasteur,* which Gallé created to celebrate the great scientist's sixty-eighth birthday in 1893, offering the vase to the Ecole Normale Supérieure.

This was the era of the Sâr Péladan and of the publication of Schuré's *Les Grands Initiés;* also the time when Freud was probing the human being's greatest depths for the purpose of demonstrating the importance of the subconscious. An eminently cultivated man, Gallé did not remain unaware of these currents of thought. He too thirsted for authenticity, seeking in all his works his own true self. In an age dominated by crass materialism, in a century utterly claimed by science and technology, Gallé endeavored to satisfy his need for revery, poetry, and spirituality. The challenge he accepted was to make glass—an ungrateful yet noble and richly plastic material—the interpreter of his dreams and aspirations (Plate 87). By doing so, he served as witness to his period's underlying sensibility; he even transcended the rationalistic reaction of the early 20th century to become the prophet and genial precursor of lyrical abstraction.

right: 88. Emile Gallé. *Bucket decorated with wine harvesters*, 1874, height 212 mm/8 1/4″, Musée de l'Ecole de Nancy. Having just opened his own glassworks, Gallé drew upon styles and techniques from the past, in this instance from the German 17th and 18th centuries.

below right: 89. Emile Gallé. *Cup with angelfish*, from a design by Victor Prouvé, 1884, height 270 mm/10 1/2″, Musée de l'Ecole de Nancy. Deriving his shape from a type of goblet, Gallé combined enameling and wheel engraving for the decoration of angelfish and children riding on snails.

GALLÉ'S ARTISTIC EVOLUTION SEEN THROUGH RARE PIECES

Emile Gallé's work is marked by perpetual exploration, the best witnesses of which can be found in the dated works. These pieces form a basis for grouping others of similar inspiration or technique:

1874: *Bucket decorated with wine harvesters* (Plate 88). One of the earliest of the dated pieces, it was made at the time Gallé opened his own glassworks, revealing the artist to be still under the influence of the past, especially the 18th century.

We do not know any works by Gallé dating from 1878, but the young master's exhibition notes indicate that the year was an important one for his new research in coloring glass—research that included the *clair de lune* ("moonlight") color among others (Plate 198). At this time Gallé also exhibited one of his first adaptations of East Asian art, using freer forms.

1884: *Cigar box*, engraved with a wriggling fish (Plate 90). In a shape derived from Chinese paintbrush holders, the material imitates rock crystal. Even so, Gallé was in fact here still "emphasizing the natural qualities of glass, especially its transparency and lucidity."

Cup decorated with angelfish and children on snails (Plate 89). Made after a design by Victor Prouvé and in "material as limpid as spring water." Gallé adopted the form of a conch shell and realized a compromise between a Renaissance form and the naturalistic shape of the snail. "In 1884, the engraving is finished with the most re-

fined detail. The figures are executed as carefully as intaglio work on fine stones."

1884: *Ballade des Dames du Temps Jadis* (Plate 92). In this piece, a brush holder, Gallé began tentatively to cloud his glass with impurities in order to obtain "novel and rare effects." These were the first indications of a new stage, wherein the artist would contradict himself by moving away from the pure, transparent material towards the manufacture of glass in several layers, colored in the mass. The engraved and enameled decoration connects it to the inscribed tankards of the 16th and 17th centuries. Bearing verses from François Villon, the work is probably one of the first *verreries parlantes* ("speaking glasses").

Vase with primulas, dedicated to Victor Lemoine (Plate 91). This piece represents in a striking way Gallé's ardent desire for aesthetic renewal, doing so through a poetic and mysterious ambience created by contrasts of light and dark, the product of streaks of oxide captured between layers of glass. Verses borrowed from Dante (*Primavera gioventù dell'anno, gioventù primavera vita;* "Spring is the youth of the year, youth the springtime of

life") underline "the interpretation of a flower motif liberated from the literal through the fruitful medium of feeling, for the purpose of decorating glass in the form of *verreries parlantes*."

The year 1884 saw an important evolution towards an increasingly personal style, a style reflecting Gallé's need to confirm his purposes by the use of inscriptions—purposes that were motivated by an eagerness to provoke thought and to establish communication with the viewer. Alert to criticism, Gallé here justified himself through reference to medieval image-makers, but he could just as well have employed inscriptions from Greek vases.

1889: *"Widerkomm" or "au revoir" vase, decorated with fleur-de-lis and "crowned chimeras"* (collection Jean Claude Brugnot, Paris). Enameled in green and red, the piece takes its novelty from the inclusion of jewellike enamels between two layers of glass.

Orpheus and Eurydice, from a design by Victor Prouvé (Plate 96). Gallé loved to provoke and exploit "accidents" during firing, in this instance turning them to special effect so that the figures seem to vanish into the internal vapors, simulated by the black streaks in the vase. "These accidents became the object of piquant games, of little Baroque problems posed to the imagination by the variegated material."

Cupid Chasing Black Butterflies (Plate 93). In this vase too Gallé made effective use of the play of light and shade.

95. Emile Gallé. *Les Carnivores* (detail), c. 1889, collection M. Périnet, Paris. *Je récolte en secret des fleurs mystérieuses* ("Secretly, I harvest mysterious flowers"). With this line from Alfred de Musset, Gallé summarized the aesthetic—a compound of the opposite demands of naturalism and symbolism—that would guide the whole of his work.

96. Emile Gallé. *Orphée et Eurydice,* after a design by Victor Prouvé, 1889, height 260 mm/10 1/8", Musée des Arts Décoratifs, Paris. From his early training, Gallé retained a taste for classical antiquity, which explains the verses engraved from Virgil. The glassmaker managed, however, to free himself from classical severity.

left: 97. Emile Gallé. *The Hydra Vase,* 1894, height 126 mm/5″, Musée du Verre, Charleroi. The hydra is enclosed in an "unfathomable" depth of material, full of air bubbles, mixed with occlusions of metal and pigment.

below: 98. Emile Gallé. (a) *The Nocturnal Butterflies,* 1898, height 281 mm/11″. Engraved with a line from Leconte de Lisle, *Echappez-vous des ombres immobiles* ("Escape from still shadows"), this vase was one of the first to be made with the *marqueterie de verre* ("glass marquetry") process, for which Gallé made a patent application on April 26 of that year. (b) *Twilight Scene,* 1898, height 203 mm/8″. A Symbolist vision of sunset, with clouds trailing on an orange ground, the poetic mood of which is enhanced by the *marqueterie* work and the lines engraved from Maurice Boucher. (c) *White Butterflies,* 1889, height 188 mm/7 1/2″. This vase marks an important stage in Gallé's career, for here he introduced "pieces of clear enameled glass in the soft paste" and thereby invented the *marqueterie de verre* process. Musée du Conservatoire des Arts et Métiers, Paris.

Vase with Moths (Plate 94). A work that may be connected with the same series.

The Carnivores (Plate 95). A verse by Alfred de Musset is inscribed below: "Secretly, I harvest mysterious flowers," which provides a kind of summary of Gallé's integrated aesthetic of those polar opposites—naturalism and symbolism. A metal foil included between two layers of glass and splintered during blowing gives this expressive piece a spontaneously mysterious quality. The ground is still semitransparent in places.

1889: *Vase with poppies* (Plate 99). The opacity of this piece derives from layers of glass strongly colored with manganese, almost to the point of blackness. The broadly worked decoration evokes that of sword guards or Japanese *inrô*. The closed poppies are dusted with various materials. This is one of Gallé's *vases de tristesse*.

right top: 99. Emile Gallé. *Vase with poppies*, c. 1889, height 155 mm/6″, private collection. The poppies folded back on themselves as on funerary urns, the black color, and even the shape of the piece all conspire to make a *vase de tristesse* ("vase of sadness"), designed in a manner to reflect Japanese influence.

right center: 100. Emile Gallé. *Nul souci de plaire* ("No desire to please"), one of Gallé's key phrases at the 1889 Universal Exhibition, height 200 mm/8″, Musée de l'Ecole de Nancy. This vase is interesting both for its theme of a toad talking to a dragonfly and for the use of acid etching on a collector's piece.

right below: 101. Emile Gallé. *La Soldanelle des Alpes* ("The Alpine Morning Glory"), c. 1892, height 110 mm/4 1/4″, Musée d'Art Moderne, Paris. The shape, the etching, and the color all contribute to the piece's symbolic qualities, which Gallé explained in his exhibition notes.

left: 102. Emile Gallé. *Le Liseron d'octobre* ("The October Bindweed"), 1892, height 200 mm/8″, Musée du Conservatoire des Arts et Métiers, Paris. "The nervations of the bindweed on the base, the jade-colored stems, the grains treated like agate, the veined leaves, and even a tiny teardrop with opal reflections—it is the sadness of the last flower of the season. . . ."

above center: 103. Emile Gallé. *La Renoncule des bois* ("The Buttercup of the Woods"), c. 1892, diameter 130 mm/5″, Musée d'Art Moderne, Paris.

above right: 104. *Les Chauves-Souris* ("The Bats"), 1892, height 95 mm/3 5/8″, Kunstmuseum, Coll. Hentrich, Düsseldorf.

below: 105. Emile Gallé. *Les Veilleuses d'automne* ("Autumn Crocuses"), 1891, height 215 mm/8 1/2″, Musée d'Art Moderne, Paris. A poetic transcription of the glassmaker's state of mind, the crocuses are stylized almost to the point of abstraction.

Nul souci de plaire (Plate 100). This became a key work of the 1889 Universal Exhibition, made simply from the contrast between a blue gather and a somber ground. It seems to represent one of the first important applications of hydrofluoric acid, reworked with the wheel. Gallé depicted this dialogue between a toad and a dragonfly several times, but the vase reissued in 1900 bears the inscription *Souci de Plaire* ("Desire to please").

The White Butterflies (Plate 98c). "Done joyously," as Gallé says in the inscription, the vase, which contains broken glass introduced into the soft paste, seems already to have been formed by a new technical process christened by Gallé in 1898—*la marqueterie de verre* ("glass marquetry").

Through their great variety, these few works from 1889 prove that we are dealing with a most important formative stage: "Some naïve first efforts exhibited in 1878 . . . are outstripped by the improvements of 1889 . . . ."

1892: *The Alpine Morning Glory* (Plate 101). "This humble flower piercing the hard ice to enjoy an hour of sun and life . . ." appears on a form shaped like a seed pod or fruit of the primula family, "with its serrations reversed on the outside." The color—"amethyst crystal with a snow layer"—is the vehicle of Gallé's Symbolist intentions.

The Buttercup of the Woods (Plate 103). In "an intaglio study of its strangely marbled leaf, spotted with white and black, like a reptile," the color itself is that of a leaf. Gallé's imagination has led him to "stress the resem-

left: 106. Emile Gallé. *La Source* ("The Spring"), 1898, height 90 mm/3 1/2″, width 250 mm/9 7/8″, collection Manoukian, Paris. The impurities in the material help to suggest stones, moss, and the bubbling of the spring.

below: 107. Emile Gallé. *Le Baumier* ("The Balsam Tree"), 1895, height 460 mm/18″, Musée d'Art Moderne, Paris.

right: 108. Emile Gallé. *The Onion Flowers*, height 482 mm/ 19″, Musée d'Art Moderne, Paris. Made by the *marqueterie de verre* technique, "for my barn display window at the Exhibition of 1900."

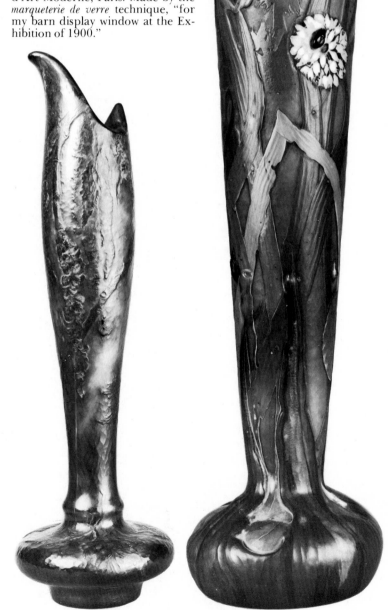

blance to a dragonfly that, half-beast, half-plant, flies in the night . . . watching his prey." An impression of calm and silence, "as in sleepy ponds under trees," emanates from this vase.

Drawings indicate that Gallé called the two pieces just cited *vases de tristesse* ("vases of sadness") to express his sometimes melancholy mood.

1892: *The October Bindweed* (Plate 102). In a still more evocative piece, Gallé used a thin but muddy palette to seize and unveil his most secret intentions. "On an ipomea limb with sensuously veined leaves, a droplet with opal lights, streaks in the late-rising fog . . . the last calyx of the season shivers at its heart. This distress implores the dim sun . . . ." To anyone who plucks it, the bindweed murmurs Verlaine's line: *Vous vous êtes penché sur ma mélancholie*.

1892: *Autumn Crocuses* (Plate 105). In "transparent crystal clouded with celestial blue and changing pinks," this work too evokes melancholy. The design grows indistinct where it encounters patches of color, resulting in a pure and poetic transcription of the glassmaker's state of mind. In its clarity of shape and its nearly abstract decoration, this vase represents an advance, not only in relation to its own time, but even in relation to Gallé's work of ten years later.

The Bats (Plate 104). The abstract tendencies of the decoration confirm that Gallé has now mastered technique and placed it in the service of his artistic and poetic demands.

1894: *The Hydra Vase* (Plate 97). This heterogeneous glass encloses a hydra in its "unfathomable" material of deep colors.

1895: *The Balsam Tree* (Plate 107). The floral shape is "designed to receive the branches of the balsam tree, which flowers in April." Covered with buds, the bronze-green material vibrates and sings through its metallic inclusions. The vase recalls "the solemn instant . . . the eternal hour, when nature is grave and maternal," according to Gallé's friend, Robert de Montesquiou.

1898: *The Nocturnal Butterflies* (Plate 98a). This was one of the first applications of "marquetry" proper, a technique Gallé was to elaborate above all others. The butterflies have "escaped from still shadows."

Twilight Scene (Plate 98b). Maurice Boucher's verses underline the evocation of a symbolic vision: *Or voici le crépuscule solitaire, son manteau violet traîne à l'horizon* ("Now comes the solitary twilight, with its violet mantle trailing on the horizon"). A flowering branch in elegant *marqueterie* is thrown negligently across the form.

1898: *The Spring* (Plate 106). The many impurities mixed with pebbles and with cabochons imitating stones seem carried along by the silvery water, "so essential, humble, precious, and chaste." Borrowing a quotation from Saint Francis of Assisi, Gallé invites the viewer to meditate upon the benefits of water: *Loué sois-tu, Seigneur, à cause de notre soeur l'eau. . . .* ("Praised be the Lord, for

right: 111. Emile Gallé. *Les Lys* ("The Lilies"), 1900, height 300 mm/11 3/4″, collection Neess, Frankfurt. The flower fades in all its baroque splendor; as re-created by the magician of glassmaking, it is ideally beautiful.

far right: 112. Emile Gallé. *Vase with poppies*, 1900, height 230 mm/9″, collection J.-Cl. Brugnot, Paris. "A flower calyx avid for air and daylight, an anthology of flowering. Yes, material, shape, coloring, and truthful decoration come from the realities of nature, that marvelous evoker of things unseen—those certainties."

below: 113. Emile Gallé. (a) *La Pervanche* ("The Periwinkle"), 1900, height 105 mm/4″; (b) *L'Anémone sylvestre* ("The Woodland Anemone"), 1900, height 180 mm/7″. Collection J.-Cl. Brugnot, Paris. Both pieces are masterful demonstrations of Gallé's *marqueterie de verre* technique.

far left: 114. Emile Gallé. *Calice-fleur colchiques* ("Autumn Crocus Calyx-Chalice"), May 2, 1898, and May 2, 1903, height 360 mm/ 14¼", private collection. Around the turn of the century Gallé moved towards sobriety and simplification.

left above: 115. Emile Gallé. (a) *Libellules* ("Dragonflies"), 1904, height 260 mm/10 1/8". This frequently repeated theme is reduced here to a silhouette, which detaches itself like a Chinese shadow from a warm-colored ground. (b) *Iris Calyx Vase*, 1901, height 350 mm/13 3/4". Marked *Étude,* this "sculpture-vase" suffered damage during manufacture but was kept as a record or "study." Musée du Conservatoire des Arts et Métiers, Paris.

left below: 116. Emile Gallé. *Pearly white crystal flagon with myosotis* ("mouse ears" or forget-me-nots), 1903, height 510 mm/20", collection J.-Cl. Brugnot, Paris. Engraving on an opaline ground, with a wrought-iron mount.

117. Emile Gallé. *La Giroflée de muraille* ("The Wallflower"), 1900, height 200 mm/7 7/8", private collection.

our sister, water. . . ."). The fervent nature-lover is fully present in works like this.

1900: *The Onion Flowers* (Plate 108). Inscribed "for my barn display window at the Exhibition of 1900," this work is a technical masterpiece, with the *marqueterie* lines mixing, crossing, and merging in a seemingly un-planned tangle.

The Woodland Anemone and *The Periwinkle* (Plate 113). Both works are moving in their simplicity, but the first especially expresses the idealist mission Gallé set himself—"to calm men."

Vase with poppies (Plate 112). "A flower calyx avid for air and daylight, an anthology of flowering. Yes, material, shape, coloring, truthful decoration all come from the realities of nature, that marvelous evoker of things unseen—those certainties."

1900: *The Iris* (Plate 109), *The Orchid* (Plate 110), and *The Wallflower* (Plate 117). All are works influenced by Symbolism and nature, works in which Gallé disdained the minutiae of composition, presenting only the mass of the object as a whole, in a powerfully evocative way.

The Tadpoles (Plate 118) and *The Beetle* (Plate 119). This pair form part of a strange symbolic bestiary that Gallé created with all the fervor and enthusiasm seen above.

All of Gallé's works from this time on are associated with dreams. All are symbolic. This is why Louis de Fourcaud

118. Emile Gallé. *Les Têtards* ("The Tadpoles"), 1900, height 317 mm/12 1/2", private collection. This elegant cornet shape bears lines from Théophile Gautier.

below: 119. Emile Gallé. *Le Scarabée* ("The Beetle"), 1900, height 242 mm/9 1/2″, private collection. In the ancient world this strange little creature symbolized immortality. Like the Egyptians, Gallé "discovers beyond appearances the reflection of an august image . . . a witness rendered . . . to the existence of God the creator . . . ." (Admission speech at the Académie Stanislas in 1900.)

compares the master to Puvis de Chavannes: "Gallé's mood leads him frequently to choose an opaline or milky, mat material in pearly whites, light blues, dull greens, faded yellows, and soft rose tones, which come close to the style of Puvis de Chavannes' painting for the staircase of the Hôtel de Ville. The painter-glassmaker of the interior dream catches up in his own way with the great painter of human serenity. This spiritual harmony in modern French art marks the year 1900."

1901: *Iris Calyx Vase* (Plate 115b). A "sculpture-vase," rendered symbolically expressive through stylization.

1903: *The Dragonfly* (Plate 120). This recurrent theme in Gallé's art is here made an integral part of the vitreous mass. Seized during its flight above the marshes, the fantastic dragonfly attains the importance of a sign. It is, however, made convincingly real by the rosy drops delicately placed on its wings. The creature has traveled a long way from the enameled dragonflies in Plates 157 and 158, where the search was mainly for harmony of decoration and shape, and much less for content or symbolic meaning.

Autumn Crocus Calyx-Chalice (Plate 114). This is another example of the sobriety and simplification towards which Gallé seemed to be moving more and more.

Pearly white crystal flagon (Plate 116). This vessel seems encased in noble armor, evoking in its own way, perhaps better than a poem would, the proud knight who protects the frail young girl of his thoughts.

left: 120. Emile Gallé. *The Dragonfly*, 1903, height 260 mm/10 1/8″, collection Manoukian, Paris. The recurring theme of the dragonfly is here incorporated in the vitreous mass, with only the globular eyes standing out from the background. What a long way Gallé had come from the enameled dragonflies of his early works! See Plate 158.

right: 121. Emile Gallé. *Pine Trees*, 1904, height 180 mm/7″. One of the artist's last works, this piece suggests the mysterious soul of the forest. Until the end of his life, Gallé sought to express the emotion he felt before the inexhaustible spectacle of nature.

Gallé now felt less need to explain his works with verses. The pieces simply speak for themselves through their colors—delicate or cold, strange or morbid. He knew how to utilize every possibility for generating mystery, how to create works at once disconcerting and attractive, and unexpected in their details.

1904: *Pine Trees* (Plate 121). In this vase Gallé has succeeded in portraying the mystery and soul of the forest. He did so by means of the simple play of decoration against two encasing layers of glass, and by means of light and shade set off by an opaline ground.

1904: *Dragonfly Cup* (Plate 115a). Here the dragonfly is but a silhouette that, like a Chinese shadow, stands out from the pale ground.

Le Lis ("The Lily Tankard-Vase"), Musée de l'Ecole de Nancy. Dedicated "to Louis de Bousles de Fourcaud, with every affection of spirit and heart," this is a culminating work, in which deep cutting conveys the depth of feeling. The handle is metamorphosed into a splendid fleur-de-lis.

Over the years, through his work, the contemporaries of Gallé were able to follow the progressive expansion of the artist's personality and his inexhaustible capacity for self-renewal. It is easy to see why Gallé generated consternation as well as enthusiasm by his way of "holding the inert material in subjection, forcing it to acknowledge the glassmaker's scepter and obey the magic wand of the sorcerer, who makes it a slave to his fantasy."

above left: 122. Emile Gallé. *Vase with lily-of-the-valley*, c. 1900, height 260 mm/10 1/8″, collection A. Lesieutre, Paris.

above right: 123. Emile Gallé. *Fish Vase*, height 380 mm/15″, collection A. Lesieutre, Paris. With its carp shape and enameled fish decoration, this vase is integrated in both form and theme.

124. Emile Gallé. *Cabbage Leaf*, c. 1900, height 160 mm/6 1/4″, collection M. Périnet, Paris. Three delicately wrought butterflies are to be found engraved upon the interior surface of a thick cabbage leaf.

SOME GALLÉ SHAPES

Gallé was an inventor of shapes as well as decorations. Yet he did not neglect the shapes he had taken directly from antiquity or the Renaissance, out of which, almost despite himself, he sometimes drew "fantastic" interpretations—as he called them. So profound was his assimilation of antique forms that they seem as much the products of his imagination as of his scholarship (Plates 125, 128, 129).

Gallé never ceased searching for new and personal forms in nature (Plates 122, 123). "With singular originality, his designs for vases are gradually inspired by fauna and flora—nautilus shells, the veining of lily-of-the-valley, the trumpet of the arum lily, the corolla of the datura or the narcissus, a branch of bindweed, a stem of angelica, the unfurling of the banana tree," together with columbines (Plate 127); the corolla of the violet or the iris (Plate 139), and forms inspired by his vegetable garden: gourd, garlic, onion, tomato, artichoke (Plates 124, 126, 141). "To him everything is useful for breathing new life into the old shape formulas customary in glassmaking up to that time" (Henrivaux). His works can also take on very strange forms, such as *Hand with Seaweed* in Plate 132, where the fingers and algae are confounded in an almost surreal, phantomlike form. Is this a drowned hand from the underwater world of the legendary town of Ys? Or the hand of a shipwrecked man in distress? In its turn, a branch of

hazel becomes a ring stand, its cup holding foliage populated by ladybirds, caterpillars, and grasshoppers (Plate 140). But it was the mushroom that elicited the glassmaker's wildest and most spectacular interpretations, as in the lamp titled *Les Coprins*, of which only four examples are known (Plate 131). A high point in a major oeuvre, this work reveals its creator's artistry and spirit at their fullest. As a complete work of art, it occupies a special place in Gallé's production of lamps. And Gallé turned out many lamps (Plates 130, 133), finding them an ideal vehicle for realizing his plan to ennoble the necessities of daily life and to make art as widely accessible as possible.

While endowing his lamps with floral and vegetable forms, Gallé exploited technology to make the scintillating electric lights play an important role in the total effect. His goblets, although in more sober shapes, are no less stamped with Gallé's personal taste. Here the motifs are most likely to be artichokes, hops, or thistle.

In general, we can say that the forms invented by Gallé are never inert, but rather vital and organic, qualities produced by his principle of working from direct observation of nature, all the while that he made certain to reshape the motif in the light of his own most intimate vision. Seeking artistic equivalents rather than literal imitations, Gallé never allowed himself merely to copy a theme.

The works on this page, all in the Paris collection of J.-Cl. Brugnot, illustrate the great stylistic variety that Émile Gallé was capable of in the late part of his career.

right: 125. *Vase with ears of wheat*, c. 1900, height 305 mm/12″. Even at his most naturalistic, Gallé observed the classical ideal, here transforming an ear of wheat into a handle for a vase shape based upon Roman models.

far right 126. *Artichoke Vase*, c. 1900, height 180 mm/7″. The artichoke flowers, realized in *marqueterie de verre*, serve for a fresh and delectable creation.

below left: 127. *Columbine Vase*, c. 1898–1900, height 285 mm/11 1/8″. On a flower shape elongated into a cornet, the columbines have been worked in *marqueterie de verre*.

below center: 128. *Le Sommeil des coccinelles* ("The Sleep of Ladybirds"), c. 1900, height 240 mm/9 1/2″. Ladybirds (amethyst cabochons) sleep in blossoms wheel-carved in glass shaped like a tulip.

below right: 129. *L'Hippocampe* ("The Sea Horse"), c. 1900–04, height 305 mm/12″. A classical shape has been carved to yield up the image of a shellfish.

left: 130. Emile Gallé. *Lamp decorated with bats,* 1900, height 400 mm/15 5/8″, collection Daverio, Lausanne. The bronze mount was made in Gallé's own workshops.

below left: 131. Emile Gallé. *Les Coprins,* height 830 mm/32 5/8″, collection J.-Cl. Brugnot, Paris. Only four examples are known of this bronze-mounted "mushroom" lamp, which was commissioned for a dining room décor with a forest theme. A spectacular creation, the lamp summarizes the virtuosity, the art, and the deep thought that Gallé invested in his glass.

below right: 132. Emile Gallé. *La Main aux algues* ("The Hand with Seaweed"), c. 1900, height 270 mm/10 1/2″, Musée de l'Ecole de Nancy. A strange hand, unreal and yet expressive, it is at once a poetic statement and a glass sculpture in dazzling colors.

far left: 133. Emile Gallé. *Lamp in the shape of a corolla,* 1900, height 500 mm/19 5/8", collection J.-Cl. Brugnot, Paris. Here nature inspired a bronze-footed lamp with a highly original shape.

left: 134. Emile Gallé. *Vase decorated with iris,* c. 1895–1900, Musée des Arts Décoratifs, Paris. Executed by the goldsmith Cardeilhac, the silver mount, with its mixture of naturalism and stylization, harmonizes perfectly with the overall design of the vase.

below: 135. Emile Gallé. *Crystal vase engraved with a nymph and a fish,* c. 1889, height 255 mm/10", collection M. Périnet, Paris. *Nymphe de l'eau vive/La truite naïve/Au jeu des amours/Se prendra toujours* ("Nymph of the living water/The naïve trout/In the game of love/Will always be taken"). The wooden base as well as the vase came from Gallé's atelier, and together they make a harmonious whole. See Plates 143 and 185.

GALLÉ VASES WITH MOUNTS

Mounts were very much in vogue at the end of the 19th century, for they heightened the effect of the vases and made them appear even more precious. Since the mounts not only gave the objects greater stability but also, at times, helped to hide imperfections, the fashion was both decorative and utilitarian. Mounts belong to a very old tradition going back to the Middle Ages and advancing through the Renaissance and the 17th and 18th centuries. During the 19th century it was customary simply to repeat old models, until, with the aesthetic renewal at the end of the period, artists gradually freed themselves from worn-out modes and formulated a contemporary style.

Emile Gallé too developed a taste for mounts, without however making it an absolute habit. In his first mounts he gave up the 18th century only with difficulty (Plate 49), for the good reason that the first artists he permitted himself to follow were those who had long been mounting vases made at Sèvres or in China. It should not surprise us, therefore, to find that even for his most advanced work, Art Nouveau in style and completely free of all academic constraint, he could allow tradition to govern the mounts (Plate 146).

Soon, however, the mounts would match the design of the vase and actually complete it (Plate 134). The support becomes an integral part of the piece, depicting waves, rocks, seaweed, even snails and dragonflies (Plate 137). Aquatic growths can grow out of the base, climb the vase, and then tumble over its shoulder or neck (Plate 138).

far left: 136. Emile Gallé. *Vase with wheel-carved orchid*, May 2, 1876, and May 2, 1901, height 200 mm/7 7/8″, private collection. Emile Falize, one of the age's finest goldsmiths, created a bronze mount from which ears of wheat grow out of their sheaves and climb over the vase's swelling volume. Engraved by wheel: *Ecoutez la chanson triste/Qui ne pleure que pour vous* ("Listen to the sad song/That weeps only for you"). To reinforce the mood, an opal tear runs down the vase.

left: 137. Emile Gallé. *Vase decorated with a marqueterie iris*, c. 1900, height 390 mm/15 1/2″, private collection.

below left: 138. Emile Gallé. *Amphora*, 1900, height 1 m/39 1/2″, Musée de l'Ecole de Nancy. Marcel Schwob's story, *Le Livre de Monelle*, inspired this huge vase, whose powerful mount became integral with the lower part of the piece. For the marriage of M. Cobrin of Nancy.

right: 139. Emile Gallé. *La Violette*, 1900, height 180 mm/7″, private collection. After choosing the verse—*La violette n'étant pas plus modeste que le pavot* ("The violet, no more modest than the poppy")—Gallé transformed it into a sumptuous corolla, made even more splendid by patination and *marqueterie de verre*.

right center: 140. Emile Gallé. *Ring stand*, c. 1880–84, height 200 mm/8″, collection J.-Cl. Brugnot, Paris. A branch of hazel becomes a filigreed crystal ring stand, imprisoning insects in its cup filled with enameled flowers.

The mounts of wood, bronze, or wrought iron were, for the most part, made in the Gallé workshops, under the master's direction (Plate 135). For those in silver or vermeil, however, Gallé turned to some of the great goldsmiths of his time—Emile Falize, Froment-Meurice, Gérard Sandoz, Guerchet, Cardeilhac, and Bonvallet, to cite only the most famous. Falize was one of the first engravers to reproduce a somewhat stylized vegetal decoration in which the new trend could be sensed. He made supports for a number of Gallé's vases. Using shapes invariably borrowed from nature, Falize loved to reproduce a plant in all its details (Plate 136). His style is always distinguished and fine, if occasionally a little thin. On the other hand, Bonvallet took from nature only the lines or forms that would create a continuity of style from the mount to the vase, the better to make them seem a single, unified work of art. He simplified his themes, then styled them with breadth and amplitude. As for the other goldsmiths, they generally found it difficult to free themselves from the past. The most supple and the most "baroque" mounts came from the fertile reveries, sensibility, and imagination of Emile Gallé (Plates 138, 139, 143).

far right above: 141. Emile Gallé. *Ail* ("Garlic"), *Courge* ("Winter Squash"—rotting), *Tomate* ("Tomato"), and *Maïs* ("Corn"), c. 1900, private collection. Gallé transformed the products of his vegetable garden into original works of art.

right below: 142. Emile Gallé. *Beer service*, c. 1885–90, collection J. Lorch, Paris. Enriching this classically formed beer service are imitation stone cabochons and the thematically perfect leaves and flowers of hop, executed in enamel.

143. Emile Gallé. These vases together show the astonishing diversity of technique, shape, and decoration that Gallé used to create his art glass. By consistently producing work of such range and quality, Gallé entered the elite ranks of the very greatest of the 19th-century glassmakers.

GALLÉ'S FRIENDS

Through his writings and, above all, through his works, Emile Gallé became the spokesman for a certain elite whose support, understanding, admiration, and encouragement meant much to him. The associates he could most count upon were, undoubtedly, Robert de Montesquiou, Roger Marx, and, more concretely, his collaborator and friend, Victor Prouvé.

ROBERT DE MONTESQUIOU-FEZENSAC (1855–1921) An aesthete and poet, Comte Robert de Montesquiou attached himself to Emile Gallé, becoming his faithful and generous friend. Beginning in 1887, they carried on an extensive correspondence.* While Gallé engraved Montesquiou's poetic images on his vases, the latter dedicated some of his poems to the glassmaker, most notably *Les Hortensias bleus* (1896). Like Gallé, Montesquiou was a fervent admirer of Grandville and Baudelaire, and he even liked to compare the "boyish" spirit of Grandville with that of Gallé. Montesquiou shared the period's love of Japanese art and had his collection *Les Chauves-Souris* ("The Bats," 1892) illustrated by the Japanese artist Yamamoto. Finding the texts all but "engraved in onyx or simulated amethyst," Gabriele d'Annunzio drew an analogy between them and the "forged glass" of Gallé (Plates 68, 104).

Montesquiou's friendship, which was based upon mutual empathy and shared tastes, certainly had considerable influence upon Gallé. Was it not Montesquiou who persuaded Gallé to visit Bayreuth, the home of Cosima and Richard Wagner, the great creator of myths and symbols? It seems that, above all else, Gallé would have seen in Montesquiou a certain Baudelairian ideal, composed of subtleties, refinements, a love of color and fragrance, an appreciation of rare and strange sensations.

Montesquiou also introduced Gallé to Marcel Proust. In *A la Recherche du Temps Perdu*, Proust refers to Gallé several times: *La mer . . . effilochait sur toute la profonde bordure rocheuse de la baie des triangles empennés d'une immobile écume linamentée avec la délicatesse d'une plume ou d'un duvet dessinés par Pisanello, et fixés par cet email blanc, inaltérable et crémeux qui figure une couche de neige dans les verreries de Gallé.* ("The sea . . . broke up, along the entire rocky shore of the bay, into feathered triangles of still foam, soft as a plume or down drawn by Pisanello and fixed in that eternal creamy whiteness representing a blanket of snow in glass made by Gallé.") Or again: *Bientôt l'hiver; au coin de la fenêtre, comme un verre de Gallé, une veine de neige durcie.* ("Soon winter; in the corner of a window, as on a glass by Gallé, a frozen strip of snow.") In 1900 an historian even compared Proust's phrase, *en un français flexible, flottant, enveloppant en échappements infinies de couleurs et de nuances, mais toujours translucide* ("in a flexible and floating French, enveloping colors and shading in an infinite elusiveness, yet always translucent"), to the *verreries où Gallé enferme parfois ses baves* ("glass works where Gallé encloses his frothings").

A common harmony of expression explains the admiration felt by both Proust and Montesquiou for Gallé. Frequently, Proust offered "Gallé" vases to his friends. In 1897 the names of Gallé and Montesquiou appeared side by side on the manifesto of the so-called *cent quatre*. Launched on the initiative of Proust, this document of the "hundred and four" called for a review of the trial of Alfred Dreyfus.

ROGER MARX (1859–1913) Speaking of Roger Marx, Gallé called him "the most passionate advocate of the rehabilitation of the decorative arts." Marx, a fellow native of Nancy, was one of the first to encourage Gallé. In 1883 he became art critic for the journal *Le Voltaire* and editor-in-chief of the *Gazette des Beaux-Arts*. From the time of the 1889 Universal Exhibition, he made Gallé known through a series of laudatory articles. For the 1900 Universal Exhibition he organized the section devoted to the decorative arts, and the success it achieved was owing in great part to the organizer's enthusiastic dedication. Marx, like Gallé, believed that art must serve as a means of achieving union among men. In love with the ideal, Marx understood and admired Emile Gallé, who had put just such aspirations into practice.

Marx was, moreover, a great collector of Gallé's works, but the collection was dispersed at public auction shortly after his death in 1914. Witnessing the event, Anatole France wrote at the time: "All that Roger Marx had admired was there."

---

*Philippe Jullian, *Robert de Montesquiou ou un Prince 1900* (1963, p. 113).

VICTOR PROUVÉ (1858–1943) Gengoult Prouvé, Victor's father, had been a modeler-ceramist in the studio of Charles Gallé, and one of the first to bring new life to the faïence works of Saint-Clément. "Born," as Henrivaux wrote, "with drawing charcoal and a roughing chisel in his hand," Victor soon found himself in contact with Emile Gallé, even becoming the glassmaker's best friend. Already gifted at the age of twelve, Victor Prouvé produced for Saint-Clément a faïence "farm" service animatedly decorated with chickens, dogs, and cocks.

While young, Gallé and Prouvé became close through their shared taste and ideals, which centered upon the search for beauty and the love of nature. From 1874, when Gallé took over the studios from his father, Victor Prouvé was entrusted with making glass eyes for a famous series of cats. A clever draftsman, he later did the drawings for vase decorations incorporating human figures, then those for designs to be executed in marquetry and sculptured furniture. Also to Prouvé must go credit for the designs of several outstanding vases, among them the celebrated *Orpheus and Eurydice* (96), *Night, Silence, Sleep,* and *Cupid Chasing Black Butterflies* (Plate 93). For the most part these are works devoted to mythological subjects.

In 1892 Prouvé painted a portrait of Emile Gallé, and no artist could have been better prepared to express the unique personality of the great glassmaker, who is represented at his work table in the heat of creative endeavor.

Prouvé shared with Gallé the same ideas on the role of the artist in society, his role as educator and propagator of beauty in everyday life, as the "missionary of the interiors" in modern cities. And did not these ideas form the very foundation of the Ecole de Nancy, of which Prouvé was vice-president and then, in 1904, president, after the death of Gallé?

When Victor Prouvé was admitted to the Legion of Honor in 1896, Gallé created a vase for the occasion and offered it to his associate: "The vase I have made for my brave friend . . . overworked for so long . . . . Innocence, patience, sobriety, goodness, simplicity, proud timidity, modesty, and humility before the grandeur of exalted ideal—such was the virtue that must now be acknowledged."

But there were other personalities who partook of the "great work." As we have seen, Tokouso Takasima contributed his native Oriental culture. After traveling in Europe as the representative of his country, Japan, Takasima became a student at Nancy's Forestry School, where he remained from 1885 to 1888, during which time he joined with Gallé and his friends. A painter and watercolorist, Takasima exhibited in Nancy. At the Musée de l'Ecole de Nancy, one can still see his work, in which the preferred motifs are biological, treated in the Japanese manner.

Lending great moral support to the Gallé enterprise were Jules Henrivaux and Louis de Fourcaud. "I thank you for all your kindness and warm-heartedness towards an isolated artist, given while you were a big industrialist," wrote Gallé to Fourcaud in a farewell letter of 1904.

Emile Gallé also had numerous friends, both known and unknown, who were able to sustain him in an ambience conducive to his development. In showing their confidence, they helped him create what he held closest to his heart—the Ecole de Nancy.

96

TECHNIQUES GALLÉ PUT AT THE SERVICE OF HIS EXPRESSION

In the presence of a finished work of art we tend to think only of the inspired moment and its poetic transposition, forgetting all the research and technical effort required for its realization. With Gallé, however, the processes were so numerous and so varied that it is not possible to ignore them, much less to enumerate them all. Using every known technique, he most often enriched materials and procedures through his own sense of their expressive possibilities. To study them, it is necessary to analyze the coloring substances, their chemical or simply decorative effects, and the extent to which they may have been conditioned by manipulation or even atmosphere. But in glass the surprises provided by chemistry are nothing compared to the ever-present uncertainty of firing, a process with inherent imponderables that must nonetheless be taken into account. As Gallé himself phrased it: "All calculations are very often upset by unexpected happenings, but the very risks of manufacture, wherever fire is a violent and brutal collaborator, sometimes produce happy results." For us to say more would require a discussion of glassmaking in general, and such is not the purpose of this book. Here we can deal only with the techniques most often adopted by Gallé for the achievement of his own precise and quite personal goals. All bear the hallmark of an originality so striking that even the simplest of the processes would have sufficed to bring Gallé great fame.

Before continuing, we should point out that Gallé's glass is usually free-blown, which means that it does not have the regularity of molded pieces. Even when he used a mold, which was rarely the case, the pieces that came forth have the character of a work of art (Plate 144).

144. Emile Gallé. *Vase with a mythological theme*, c. 1890, height 380 mm/15″, Musée de l'Ecole de Nancy. Mold-blown, this piece has a ground of sea green.

Gallé and Enameling

Emile Gallé attached great importance to enameling and considered it one of the most interesting of all decorative processes. He began using the technique as early as 1873, and thereafter made frequent reference to it in his account of exhibitions.

"Since 1878," he said, "I have continued to ornament glass with the help of colors and enamels that are vitrifiable at low temperatures, close to the softening point. Painted and enameled decoration leaves nothing to be desired, neither charm nor effect. . . . In 1878 I exhibited relief enamels appliquéd to glass in the Japanese manner. . . . Once they had become successful to the point of overuse, I sought to renew these enamels with hitherto untried shades: various blues as well as greens and yellows of every kind, including both subtle and broken tones."

At first, Gallé limited his colors to red, white, turquoise, and opaque green, along with translucent blue and gold. For the sake of efficiency, an outline drawing of the design was brushed onto the piece in brown. This procedure resembled one used by faïence makers and called *chatironnage.* The outline sometimes became a decorative element, as it does in a vase with a shape inspired by Japanese perfume braziers (Plates 145).

The enamel palette developed by Gallé was already largely complete by the time of the 1884 Exhibition of Decorative Arts (Plate 146). Thereafter his enamels would become ever more remarkable for the richness and power of their hues (Plates 142, 147, 148, 154). Whether opaque or translucent, the master varied them infinitely: grisaille upon a ground spangled with silver or gold sandwiched between layers of glass; black cameos; lattices of gold, repainted with silver or platinum or, as it seems in a delight-

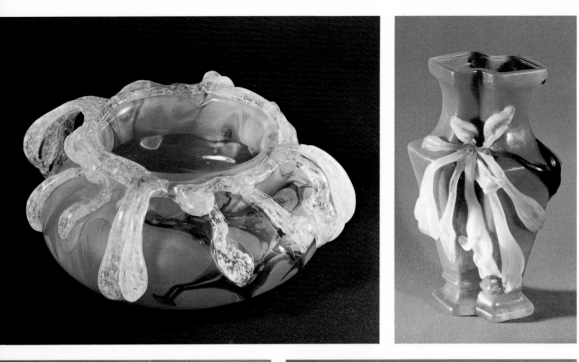

far left: 149. Emile Gallé. *Bowl with applied decoration on a marbled ground*, c. 1900, height 200 mm/8″, collection A. Lesieutre, Paris.

left: 150. Emile Gallé. *Vase with Chinese orchid*, c. 1900, height 200 mm/8″, collection J.-Cl. Brugnot, Paris. The sculptural form, the sumptuous and sensual flower applied to vitreous material imitating precious stone, and an opal sunk within the mass make a piece of extraordinarily rich effect.

left: 154. Emile Gallé. *Pitcher decorated with enameled thistles,* c. 1878–84, height 230 mm/9", collection J. Lorch, Paris.

right: 155. Emile Gallé. *Detail of the vase in Plate 120. Emaux bijoux* and other enamels allowed Gallé truly to rival nature.

below right: 156. Emile Gallé. *Small jug with stylized flowers executed in pure tin enamel.* c. 1878–80, height 160 mm/ 6 3/8", collection J. Lorch, Paris.

far left: 151. Emile Gallé. *Le Figuier,* 1900, height 250 mm/9 3/4", collection J.-Cl. Brugnot, Paris. In this new version of the piece in Plate 72, the calyx falls upon a patinated *marqueterie* foot that seems sculpted from onyx.

left center: 152. Emile Gallé. *Vase in clear crystal shaded with black,* c. 1885–90, height 230 mm/9", collection J.-Cl. Brugnot, Paris. In contrast to the butterfly's wings and the body of the dragonfly, which are wheel-engraved and enameled in black, the dragonfly's wings and the body of the butterfly are made up of small pieces of applied glass.

left: 153. Emile Gallé. *Vase decorated with foliage,* 1900, height 412 mm/ 16 1/8", private collection.

ful little jug, with applications of pure tin enamel. In the jug the effect is enchanting (Plate 156).

Also in 1884, under the influence of Joseph Brocard, Gallé "cultivated reflective colors, associating them with the hard enamels of the Arabs." Constantly innovative, he again exhibited new preparations in 1889. These were "opaque enamels in strange and bizarre tints, with broken hues adding liveliness to the middle range of a powerful color scale. He also exhibited opaque enamels that, because colored with gold preparations, yield rose and lilac tonalities," recalling Chinese enamels on *famille rose* porcelain. A cup decorated with flowers and aquatic grasses is probably from this period, although the mount belongs to the Louis XV style (Plate 146). Japanese influence appears even in the signature, which is composed of floating earthworms. Decorations inspired by Japan can also be found on shapes more directly related to Japanese art.

Relishing difficulties, Gallé adapted his translucent enamels to pieces earlier decorated with opaque enamels.

When exposed to reflected light, the resulting colors glow with a brilliant inner fire. The permanence of such enamels is a tribute to Gallé's determination to solve major technical problems. The fusion point for the decoration must be close to that of glass itself; thus, if the firing time is not carefully controlled, the object could come out deformed.

In a still bolder move, Gallé invented what he called *emaux-bijoux* ("enamel jewels"). These were translucent enamels built up in successive layers and fused to a fine metal base, which was then applied by heat to the glass piece. With the metal providing stability, the enamels could be fired at a low temperature, and this greatly extended the decorative possibilities available to the artist. After much refinement and through judicious use of this technique, Gallé could re-create the natural, living appearance of a beetle's carapace, or the eyes of a dragonfly (Plates 147, 155), or even the glinting, palpitating, diaphanous quality of wing tissue and dew drops (Plate 158).

Gallé's Champlevé Enamels

Gallé employed the term *champlevé* for an enamel process that yielded effects resembling those of champlevé enamel on copper or of 16th-century inlays on rock crystal. After cavities had been cut in the glass, and sometimes gilded in the fire, they were filled with sufficient enamel to achieve a surface level with that of the glass piece. A decoration created by this means appears to have the massiveness of a mount. If enhanced by gold insertions, the work acquires a rare sumptuousness. In the vase decorated with chrysanthemums the technique has been joined to a distinctly Oriental mood (Plate 159).

Tempted to experiment further, without however abandoning his earlier procedures, Gallé during the following years learned to apply "gouache enamels in the Chinese manner to glass porcelain." According to Henrivaux, "their subtlety of tone rises to heights attained by his earlier types." The recurrent dragonfly once again served as a decorative motif in a delicate little bowl of opaline glass, where it stands out as though on a luminous screen (Plate 157).

Before leaving this chapter on enameling, we should give further consideration to a process already encountered elsewhere—that of *verre églomisé*. This was a process wherein Gallé took painted or encrusted "enamel jewels" while still hot and encapsulated them between two layers of glass. To make the inserted forms seem integral with their container, Gallé then used a special lacquer, or sometimes he concealed the joint with a circle of gilt enamel (Plate 148). The artist acknowledged his source of inspiration for *verre églomisé* in German glass made during the 16th through the 18th centuries. Among Germans such pieces were know as *Zwischengoldgläser* or *Zwischensilbergläser*, depending upon the precious metal used for the ground—gold or silver.

Insertions of gold or platinum could be added to the enamels in the form of leaves, flakes, dust, or even drops. But Gallé insisted that "the leaves must be torn, and irregularly precise."[*] Thus, in the little bucket reproduced in Plate 148, enamels and insertions of gold are combined to create a more precious and delicate effect.

*Raymond Chambon, *Catalogue de l'Exposition du Verre à Charleroi* (Charleroi, 1970).

right: 157. Emile Gallé. *Cup with dragonfly,* c. 1890, height 145 mm/ 5 5/8″, collection Manoukian, Paris. A recurring theme throughout Gallé's work, the dragonfly here becomes a pretext for the use of "gouache enamels in the Chinese manner on glass porcelain," which makes the insect stand out from the opaline ground as if seen against a luminous screen.

below left: 158. Emile Gallé. *Smoked crystal cup with insertions of gold leaf,* 1880, height 170 mm/6 5/8″, collection Manoukian, Paris. The enameling of the butterfly and the attenuated dragonfly is very restrained.

below right: 159. Emile Gallé. *Vase with chrysanthemums,* c. 1889, height 255 mm/10″, private collection. Using what he called *champlevé,* enamels placed in grooves cut into the vitreous mass, Gallé achieved an effect resembling copper enameling, but in a style that is resolutely Oriental.

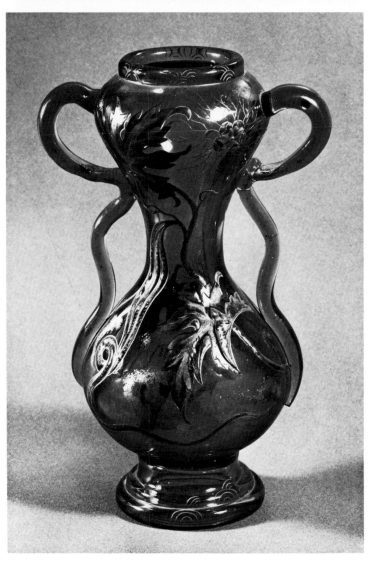

right: 160. Emile Gallé. *Vase decorated with roses*, c. 1890–1900, height 180 mm/7″, Musée de l'Ecole de Nancy. Thanks to carving with the small wheel, the rose stands out in splendid relief, its every feature modeled in exquisite detail.

below: 161. *Detail of the vase with a dragonfly in Plate 186a.* The various techniques evident here: hot-glass applications, wheel engraving in the insect wings and in the beautiful signature, and a patina to shade the ground. Gallé loved to say: "Our tools have left their form in the crystal."

Gallé's Applied Decoration

Even with the classical, timeless processes of applying decoration to molten glass, Gallé often succeeded in creating something exceptional. But, as always, he worked with brio and invention (Plate 149). The appliqué might consist of simple fragments of broken colored glass, fired to the host form and then wheel-engraved, as in the vase with the dragonfly and butterfly design in Plate 152. Or it could be an overt addition, which is the case with a series of large blossoms—orchids, roses, lilies—all appearing half-real, half-idealized as they stand forth and drape their flowing, luxuriant forms around the body of whatever piece they adorn (Plates 110, 111, 150). "With nature's own grace, the applied flower seems to emerge from the depths of the material, its parts adding relief to the object it decorates. Fine carving done with a small wheel has shaped the contours and revealed the delicate nervation of petals."*

Sometimes the applied material draws attention to itself by streaming down in white runnels all over the vase (Plate 149). At other times the glass layers are juxtaposed, soldered, or applied one over the other to form a single work of rich and original appearance (Plates 72, 151).

Most often engraving with a small wheel has been used to finish the applied ornament, which can be found on works cased in several layers, enhanced with *marqueterie*, patinated, acid-etched, or treated in any other way that might serve the single purpose of endowing the final piece with an ever stronger sense of life (Plates 112, 113, 127–129, 153, 160, 161). It must be understood, however, that Gallé never exploited his formidable technical powers for mere virtuoso display.

*Emile Nicolas, *La Lorraine* (January 1901).

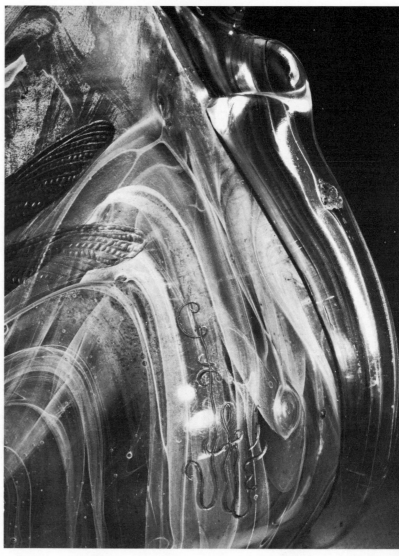

162. Emile Gallé. *Cup decorated with moths,* c. 1889–92, height 90 mm/ 3 1/2″, diameter 170 mm/6 5/8″, private collection. Wheel engraving of the various layers of rose and jade crystal has attained a rare perfection, both on the interior and on the exterior of the vase, lending depth and dynamism to the decoration—a swarm of insects.

Gallé's Engraving and Etching

"The simultaneous practice of all known processes for engraving crystal, from carving with the grinding wheel, or even 'chiseling' with the cutting wheel, to acid baths and the diamond point, offers a highly varied picture of this art. In the glyptic works, I have used every possible resource: patinas, lusters, mat finishes, grains that are soft to both touch and eye, low reliefs, cameos, outer layers in high relief, and under layers creating the effect of stained-glass windows, the modeling done with cutting wheels of the smallest possible diameter." Finding the standard engraver's tools insufficient, Gallé invented a vertical lathe for carving heavy crystal and extremely hard, potassium-based glass.

Wheel Engraving In his book *Le Verre et le Cristal,* Jules Henrivaux, director of Saint-Gobain, wrote that "very early in his career, M. Gallé tried to win back a special, small public for an art that had shone brightly in antiquity, as well as in the 16th and 17th centuries—the art of engraving on glass, with or without enamels. In public taste, color had, in fact, completely eclipsed the charming art of engraving." When, therefore, Gallé in 1878 made and exhibited *The Four Seasons,* a small cup with motifs taken from Raphael and engraved as well as enameled, he did so to "rekindle decoration."

Up to 1884 the engraving was done either with a small emery wheel or with lead, copper, or wooden wheels, and "carried to the most precious finish, with the figures executed as carefully as intaglio work on fine stones." But, ever concerned about quality, Gallé wanted to avoid making hard, cold works, like some fine stones whose engraving displays nothing but a specialist's manual dexterity.

Here, as everywhere, Gallé sought a means of expression, and preferred to allow technical imperfections if these could prevent an impression of dryness, boredom, or monotony. So that his forms would not look like castings or reproductions, he loosened control over certain secondary elements. But the greatest source of aesthetic vitality came from the artist's own love and respect for his material. All these views, which were published in 1889, remained true for the whole of Gallé's work. The pieces to which he wanted to give the most striking appearance were completed and reworked with the wheel (Plate 163). Thus, the objects retain the charm of the unexpected at the same time that they also possess a distinctly individual character. When wheel engraving was not the chief decorative means, it became a finishing element.

Gallé achieved his most beautiful decorative effects by engraving on vases of cased glass—that is, works constructed of several superimposed layers of vitreous materials, each in a different color. Using wheels of several sizes and varying their speed of rotation, the craftsman could cut into and carve the layers, penetrating them to lesser or greater depths, so as to reveal one color or another (Plate 113). In a letter of 1890 to one of his collaborators (Chambon), Gallé wrote that the relative depth of his cutting enabled him to "obtain a very sober, beautiful brown in the thicker passages and, by contrast, a transparent shell color in the thinner layers." Here he was writing of two-layered glass. In the instance of glass with three or four superimposed colors, the cutting could produce multiple and unexpected planes, with deep or shallow modeling, or subtly gradated, blended tones, all evincing the engraver's skill and artistic sensibility (Plates 153, 177a).

right: **163.** Emile Gallé. *Vase with French roses,* c. 1900, height 440 mm/
17″, collection K. Gunther, Frankfurt. The roses appliquéd to the
ground become a beautifully wrought garland.

below: **164.** Emile Gallé. *Vase with orchids,* c. 1895–1900, height 210
mm/8 1/4″, private collection. The wheel-engraved flower retains its
mystery, in considerable part because the occlusions from which it
emerges can be detected only with the aid of a special light.

The famous *Portland Vase** in the British Museum offers
a classic example of this process. Decorated by an ancient
two-layer technique—opaque white on blue-black—it has
the appearance of a true cameo. Indeed, for a long time
experts thought it was an engraved stone, so closely do the
effects approximate those of multicolored gems.

Most often, however, the results "depart considerably
from nature, yet lack neither richness nor, above all, the
unexpected." Such is the intaglio vase with a design of
Chinese rose begonias engraved on a stratum of yellow
glass under which a silver insertion makes the material
seem like agate (Plate 168), until the object has been illuminated from within, when it assumes a purple tonality
with the glowing intensity of stained glass (Plate 169). At
work here is the principle of dichroism, by which layered,
multicolored glass changes its hue according to whether it
is seen in reflected or in transmitted light. The most accomplished example of Gallé's "cameo," or cased and
carved, work may be the vase shaped like an iris bud (Plate
193), in which the artist, by means of cutting alone, created
a decoration, sharply and deeply relieved from a ground
sprinkled with colored powders included in the vitreous
mass.

In marked contrast to the bold carving just seen is the
delicate engraving on the cup covered over with a swarm

*The so-called *Portland* or *Barberini Vase* was found in the mid-16th century in a sarcopha-
gus dating from the 2nd century A.D. It remained with the Barberini family in Rome until
they sold the piece in the 18th century. Resold to the British Ambassador in Naples, it then
went to the Duchess of Portland. After auction by her estate in 1783 and then repurchase
by her son, the vase went to the British Museum in 1845.

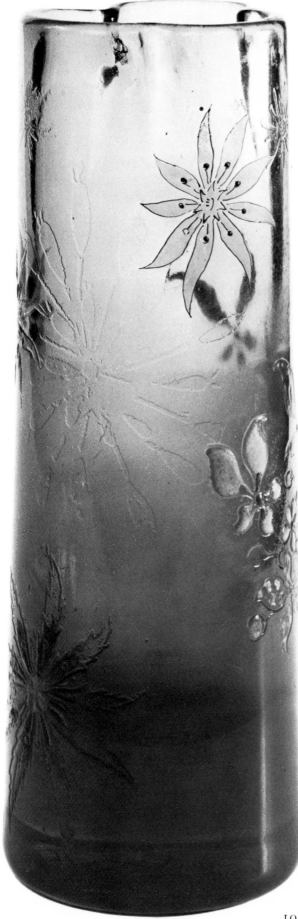

of moths (Plate 162). In response to the cup's "network of rose agate-crystal on mossy agate and jadeite glass," Jules Henrivaux concluded that, even in his most finished works, Gallé "could not go further than this prestigious tour de force." Another instance of Gallé's technical expertise can be found in a long-necked, ovoid vase engraved with orchids (Plate 164). The vase actually takes on a new artistic dimension when illumination, either with or against the light, brings out the abstract metallic inclusions, adding to the piece's mystery. Here, more than ever, the orchid is the strange flower dear to the East, a blossom whose beauty symbolizes perfection and spiritual purity.

Acid Etching Up to 1884 Gallé rejected acid etching as a decorative process, because it "neither thinks, nor adds to the model." He deemed the technique unequal to the artistic effects he sought, finding its bite too severe and too ungovernable. Yet, among other glassmakers, etching with hydrofluoric acid was a very common practice from the middle of the 19th century. Gallé used it, however, if not as a decorative means, at least as a way of preparing the grounds of his transparent glass, tinted or colorless, for subsequent enameling (Plates 165, 177b).

If, at this time, aesthetic objectives caused Gallé to prefer wheel cutting, "where there is a lively dialogue between

165. Emile Gallé. *Vase with anemones,* c. 1889, height 160 mm/6 1/4″, Musée du Verre, Charleroi. Made during a period when Gallé began using acid to lightly cut out the background of the flower decoration, or to simulate vapors or grisaille, this vase is acid-etched on both its exposed surfaces.

166 (right) and 167 (below). Emile Gallé. *Vase with columbines, mounted on bronze,* c. 1900–04, height 275 mm/10 3/4″, private collection. Under the deep bite of acid, the glass takes on the character of bark. *Marqueterie de verre* and wheel engraving were used for the flowers and leaves.

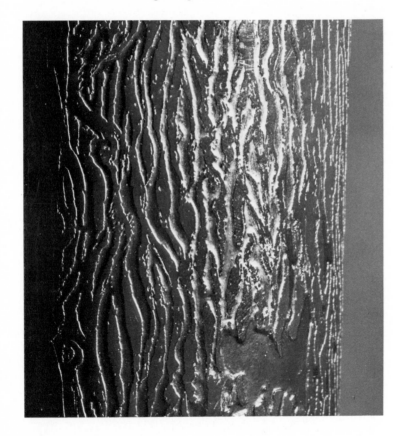

the sculptured motif and the material," in 1889 the artist recognized that acid "is appropriate for making the first cuts in certain kinds of glass." He began by applying "his savage cuts to rough out somewhat archaizing ornaments or areas in which he wanted to create a natural, unfinished look, leaving the material in what appeared to be a 'raw' state."

Acid even replaced the cutting wheel, for Gallé found that "where the wheel cannot reach, acid slides in easily." Moreover, etching proved "helpful for light and delicate ornaments, engraved with a diamond point in the protective varnish, and then cut with acid, in precise designs that have the delicacy of lace, and a fragile clarity unobtainable with any other process. Once given a grisaille patina, these designs could function as grounds against which to bring out the motif." Acid also made possible the depiction of vapors, patinas, brocading, the cellular tissues of petals, leaves, or insect and butterfly wings (Plates 84, 100, 101). This very light, evanescent quality served well to delineate the wings of a transfigured creature hovering on a burst umbel capsule, half-moth, half-dragonfly. The piece is reproduced in Plate 176.

But when Gallé wished to convince us that a formerly rejected technique could be used for highly artistic creations, and thus bent to his will, he made a fascinating vase in which, thanks to deep cutting with acid, the glass becomes a tree with a wild and rugged bark (Plate 166). Against such a ground the anemone leaves, realized in engraved *marqueterie,* stand out rather shyly. The use of *marqueterie de verre,* his most evolved technique, shows the artistic interest Gallé sought to give to this vase, a detail of which can be seen in Plate 167.

The acid-etching process is described in greater depth in the section on the Daum brothers, who excelled in its use. This illustrated discussion can be found further along, on pages 151–152.

168 and 169. Emile Gallé. *Tumbler with Chinese rose begonias,* c. 1900–04, height 170 mm/6 5/8″, collection J.-Cl. Burgnot, Paris. The flowers revealed by wheel carving in the different layers of glass have one color when viewed by reflected light (left) and yet another when seen by refracted light (right). This results from the special phenonenon called "dichroism," which Gallé learned to use expressively.

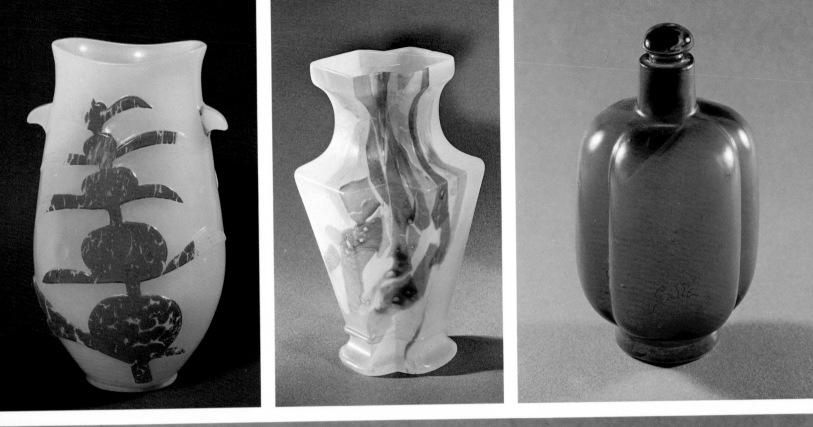

far left: 170. Emile Gallé. *Vase imitating jade,* c. 1890, height 225 mm/9″, collection A. Lesieutre, Paris. Inspired by jades brought from Peking's Summer Palace, with an agatelike flowering branch styled in the manner of Oriental ideograms.

center left: 171. Emile Gallé. *Vase imitating rose quartz,* 1890, height 235 mm/9 1/4″, collection J.-Cl. Brugnot, Paris. A ribbon of paste unfurled in the hot vitreous mass has hardened to simulate the imperfections natural to quartz, yielding a decorative effect that, like the vase's shape, shows the influence of Japan.

left: 172. Emile Gallé. *Flagon in imitation amber,* c. 1889–92, height 130 mm/5″, Musée de l'Ecole de Nancy. So perfect is the amberlike substance and so pure the Chinese snuffbox shape that alone they constitute sufficient decoration.

below left: 173. Emile Gallé. *Vases imitating amethyst,* 1889–95, Musée des Arts Décoratifs, Paris. The vase on the left is rich in technical variety: *marqueterie de verre,* appliqués, and, on the interior, acid etching.

below: 174. Emile Gallé. *Vase imitating a pink tree-agate,* c. 1890–95, height 150 mm/6″, private collection. Wheel engraving helps accentuate the effects of both the dense paste material and the mossy floral forms visible through it.

right: 175. Emile Gallé. *Vase of agated glass,* c. 1889, height 230 mm/9″, collection J.-Cl. Brugnot, Paris. Colored streams and streaks included in the vitreous mass give the vase its agatelike appearance, while an appliquéd tear of "sap" threatens to flow down the full length of the vase.

left: 176. Emile Gallé. *Capsule d'ombelle* ("Burst Umbel Capsule"), c. 1889, height 120 mm/4 5/8″, collection J.-Cl. Brugnot, Paris. With a judicious use of acid etching, Gallé simulated the cellular tissue of a dragonfly's wings.

below: 177. Emile Gallé. (a) *Vase with satin-flowers,* c. 1890, height 212 mm/8 1/4″; (b) *Vase with daisies,* c. 1890, height 120 mm/4 5/8″. Musée des Arts Décoratifs, Paris. Technique endows each of these pieces with its special qualities: wheel engraving on the left and chemical etching on the right, where traces of acid still shine.

Acid Etching and Industrial Production Along with his artistic works, Gallé was determined to sponsor a long series of industrially produced works, deliberately priced to accommodate modest budgets. "I wanted," he said in 1889, "to make art accessible in such a way as to prepare a less restricted number of people for more difficult works. I spread a feeling for nature, for the grace of flowers and the beauty of insects." From 1884 he began to study decorations that, because suitable to execution with acid, could be popularized. Conceived from simplified models, but nonetheless charming and not without artistic merit, examples of the resulting manufacture were presented at the Universal Exhibition of 1889, side by side with the master's "refined and luxurious works," whose high-quality workmanship precluded production in quantity.* In the new series he avoided "the false, the misshapen, the fragile, and used solid colors."

Thanks to the simplicity of their design and execution, the industrial pieces escaped vulgarity (Plates 178, 179), a weakness into which many mass-produced objects fell at this time, largely because of industrialists who cared little for quality or good taste. But with Gallé the industrial production must be considered as integral with his major work, in the same way that a signed lithograph belongs to the oeuvre of a painter. Gallé's mass-produced glass also has historical interest, for in it one can discern the beginnings of a democratization of art.

*Certain of these pieces can be exceptionally "brilliant units." In general, however, Gallé himself executed three or four examples so as to discover the extent of the ever-present risk of accidents, mainly in the course of firing. Designer of these models, Gallé also supervised the various stages of production, which was carried out in accordance with his personal directives.

178. Emile Gallé. *Vase with aquatic plants,* after 1890, height 160 mm/ 6 1/4″, Musée de l'Ecole de Nancy. Although mass-produced, this bowl has genuine artistic qualities, a perfect match of decoration to shape.

179. Emile Gallé. *Vase with clematis,* after 1890, height 230 mm/9″, collection H. Lorch, Paris. Etched with acid, this vase, whose form evokes a flower, illustrates Gallé's principle: make art accessible to all, without falling into vulgarity.

Although praiseworthy, Gallé's ambition led to a gradual transformation of his craft studios into a real factory, where a somewhat high-speed and large-scale fabrication exceeded the original, carefully conceived objectives. The same themes were often reworked, and the color range, especially after 1900, remained rather limited.

As we have seen, Gallé's son-in-law took over the many models created during the master's lifetime. Some authorities believe that works made after these models, up to 1914, carry a star beside the signature, but there is no certainty of this. Interpreted by some of Gallé's students, they can have a certain charm, and whatever else they may be, the pieces remain a living reflection of a fascinating period (Plate 180). After 1914, and up to the final closing in 1931, the industrial production of the Gallé factory offers little of interest.

However, some early examples illustrate quite well the goal Emile Gallé had assigned himself: "the reconciliation of cheap production and art." A vase with clematis and one with aquatic plants both embody another principle, that of a decoration harmonized with the object's shape (Plates 178, 179). The later pieces (around 1906) in the Musée du Conservatoire des Arts et Métiers retain the Gallé spirit, although they lack the touch of sparkle that their original creator knew how to achieve, even in mass-produced work.

180. Emile Gallé. (a) *Vase decorated with a landscape,* 1906, height 282 mm/11"; (b) *Vase with thistles,* 1906, 151 mm/6". Musée du Conservatoire des Arts et Métiers, Paris. Made after Gallé's death, these are mass-produced pieces bearing a signature accompanied by a star.

Gallé's Special Effects

"In my production of polychrome pieces I have used, after many experiments, no less than a hundred preparations or mixtures. And by combining the processes I can obtain an infinite variety of accidents and nuances, totally unprecedented in either modern or antique glassmaking." Writing in 1889, Gallé thus pointed out all the novel effects he could induce, beyond the imitation of natural materials. There were, among other things, dramatic, scintillating cracks, the webs of small fissures called *craquelure*, colored bubbles, iridescences, metallic pearls, singeings, and even patinas. All these discoveries produced an ornamentation of an increasingly individual character, with each innovation attracting ever greater notice from the critics.

Imitation Gemstones   The glass that emerged at this time was intimately allied to the artist's deeper knowledge of natural materials. Science, especially chemistry, offered invaluable resources to glassmakers, allowing them, for instance, to reconstitute the synthesis of natural gems, whose composition became known through chemical analysis. "Hard stones, gems, and the precious accidents that make quartz, agates, ambers, and jades" were the natural materials that Gallé attempted to reproduce.

As early as 1884 Gallé announced that he was engaged in experiments to simulate quartz amethyst, but it was not until 1889 that he succeeded in making extensive application of his discoveries (Plate 173). In satisfaction of the quartz amethyst imitation he sought, Gallé used manganese oxide as a colorant, turning the vitreous material to a brilliant or dull violet according to whether "the base is sodium or potassium." Gallé clouded, marbled, jas-

pered, jaded, ambered, and agated his glass, but whatever the process, he never failed to add his personal touch, as in the vase now owned by the Musée des Arts Décoratifs, in which shells and starfish raise the piece well above the simple imitation of a gemstone (Plate 173 right).

With a mixture based upon copper oxide or "purple of Cassius," Gallé obtained soft shades of rose quartz, so characteristic of a twin vase in which a ribbon of glass paste unfurls to make a more convincing simulation of natural defects (Plate 171). Special preparations, incorporated while hot and placed in the molten mass—always in accordance with a preconceived design—provide the internal network of streaks and veins, the "marblings" and "specklings" normally found in quarried stone. It was such a procedure that yielded the "tree-moss agate" exemplified by a charming little vase formed of dense rose-colored agate translucent enough to reveal within its depths a kind of mossy growth, to which effect wheel engraving brought accent, subtlety, and refinement (Plate 174).

To imitate onyx or sardonyx, which are agates of one or more naturally formed colored layers, Gallé included ribbons of colored paste in the vitreous mass (Plate 151). The result can be seen in a vase with a sober, slender, shape bearing a decoration formed of falling "tears" (Plate 175). The piece was one of a series of flower vases designed by Gallé in 1889.

Finally, to simulate the jades so dear to the Far East, Gallé utilized different colors in sequence, starting with a base of opaline glass, which was then tinted green with "variable proportions of potassium bichromate and copper or iron oxides." "To avoid vulgarity," Gallé wrote, "the green shade must not be too pronounced. On the other hand, imperial-green jade must be more saturated, and above all must result from the intermingling of colored mixtures." A successful example of pale "jade" is the vase with a shape inspired by a Far Eastern prototype (Plate 170). A most striking feature is the applied decoration with a plum-branch motif of speckled agate glass, carved like a calligraphed cypher meant to bear symbolic meaning to the initiated. It should be noted how marvelously the decoration is adapted to the shape.

Amber, a fossilized resin born of water, appealed to Gallé in a special way, whether for its beauty, or for the magical and therapeutic powers attributed to it by the ancients. In 1889 the artist exhibited some examples of his amber glass at the Universal Exhibition. The preparation was secret, utilizing a base of silver-yellow while incorporating various materials, and it allowed Gallé to obtain that "deep amber over colorless glass"* that he was employing in a variety of ways as late as 1892. To ensure the exact shade of amber, he gave a sample to his workers. A good illustration of what the master wanted can be found in a fine and simple piece fashioned like a Chinese snuff bottle (Plate 172).

*Raymond Chambon, *Catalogue de l'Exposition du Verre à Charleroi* (Charleroi, 1970).

181. Emile Gallé. *Vase with a corolla of lily-of-the-valley*, c. 1889–95, height 280 mm/11″, collection J.-Cl. Brugnot, Paris. No accident, the striking crack expresses the artist's desire to imitate certain of nature's imperfections. Here he obtained the effect by incorporating "asbestos threads and micalike spangles." The shape of the vase and its base, like the imperial-jade coloration, was inspired by the Far East.

right: **182.** Emile Gallé. *Vase decorated with a landscape*, c. 1885–89, height 235 mm/9 1/4″, collection J.-Cl. Brugnot, Paris. Gallé obtained the crackling, which recalls the work of Eugène Rousseau, by pouring cold water onto the vase in the course of working it.

right center: **183.** Emile Gallé. *Vase with floral decoration*, c. 1900, height 215 mm/8 1/2″, private collection. The stylized and almost abstract *marqueterie* flowers are immersed in a metallic firmament.

right below: **184.** *Detail of Plate 183.* The effect of a metallic fretwork was obtained by introducing insoluble materials between two glass layers during firing.

Fractures and Fissures Gallé induced cracks, either large or small, by pouring cold water onto the piece while working it. A well-known procedure, it received a personal touch from Gallé when he incorporated other techniques, such as grisaille enameling, which he applied to a vase with the rather strange shape of a Dutch tulip tree (Plate 182). The vigorously outlined decoration stands forth like a vignette.

In very thick, chunky pieces that were likely to develop real breaks rather than a decorative crackle, Gallé used asbestos threads, or micalike spangles, as a palliative. This seems to be how he obtained the rather striking cracks in material intended to simulate the natural imperfections found in certain kinds of quartz. The technique served the master well in a vase of imperial-jade glass formed after a corolla of lily-of-the-valley (Plate 181).

Bubbles, Metallic Occlusions, Fuming Colored bubbles, or bubbles with reflections, were produced in glass by the "injection of materials emitting vapors that, on contact with the crystal in the process of fusion, are able to form bubbles in the vitreous flux and to reduce themselves to iridescence, fixed to the walls of the bubbles in a thin, metallic layer." It was with this technique that Gallé, like a true alchemist, succeeded in representing underwater depths with unfathomable iridescences. One vase thus enhanced has been wheel-engraved with aquatic plants among whose climbing tendrils a stranded crab struts with great and humorous pomposity (Plate 190).

Discordant materials that are introduced between two layers of glass and do not dissolve in firing make the cornet

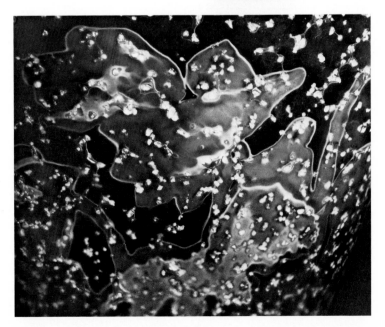

185. Emile Gallé. *Vase with a nymph,* detail of the piece in Plate 135 and in the lower left of Plate 143. Air bubbles simulating drops of water result from the "projection of materials emitting vapors that, on contact with the crystal in the process of fusion, are able to form bubbles."

vase in Plate 183 look as if it contained a starry firmament. *Marqueterie* was used to complete and enliven what became a technical tour de force (Plate 184). Gallé had yet another trick that he could apply to particularly striking effect, which was to induce "elongated air bubbles imitating boiling water" or fine drops of sparkling rain and then add aureoles of manganese oxide to endow the trapped air pockets with greater brightness (Plate 185). "The nymph of the living water,/ The naïve trout/ In the play of love/ Will always be taken," enchanting us along the way with her purity and perfection (Plates 143 lower left).

Metallic occlusions, fuming, tintings, or other metallizations could be the "product of the reducing or oxidizing action of the atmosphere in the kiln, on paraisons covered while hot with special mixtures." But Gallé knew well that the hazards of firing make it impossible to obtain two absolutely identical pieces.

Patination   As early as 1889 Gallé spoke of finishing his glass pieces by patinating them—that is, by giving them a mat, somewhat opaque, crepelike surface. He had in fact been using the effect, and extensively so, since about 1890.

Patination is a process that exploits what had always been considered a defect produced by dust from the wood or coal burned to heat the furnaces. In the course of firing, such "impure" deposits could alter the glass surface, causing it actually to devitrify—to develop blisters, "fog," pock marks, or a kind of "mousse." With his usual genius, Gallé learned to transform a technical liability into an aesthetic asset and began actually to create decorations based upon induced surface devitrification. His procedure was to expose the paraison to various ashes and dry or greasy va-

below: 186. Emile Gallé. (a) *Vase with dragonfly,* c. 1900, height 100 mm/4"; (b) *Vase with columbines,* c. 1900, height 140 mm/5 1/2". Private collection. For these pieces Gallé revealed the absolute control he had over his technical inventions, here *marqueterie de verre* and patination.

right: 187. Emile Gallé. *Detail of Plate 186b. Marqueterie de verre* permitted Gallé to heighten the decorative effect through the superimposition of layers of colored glass.

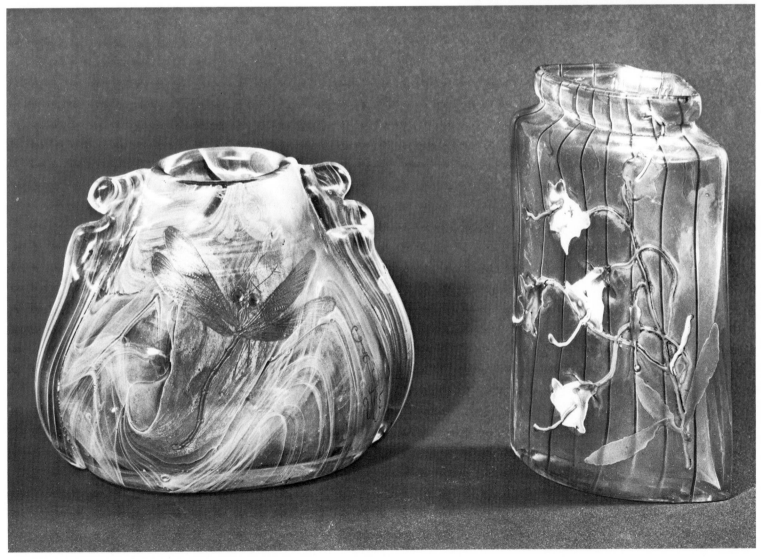

188. Emile Gallé. *Vase with magnolias,* c. 1898, height 200 mm/8″, private collection. *Marqueterie* flowers on a ground of patinated and patterned clear crystal.

pors so as to cause the surface, in whole or in part, to lose transparency, become almost opaque, and take on a dense, pumicelike texture and consistency that the master called "crystal skin" (Plate 189). This surface alteration could be initiated by rolling the paraison on a marver covered with the impurities or by blowing them upon the form through the working hole of the firing kiln. In all, the ultimate effect is governed by the chemical composition of the vitreous mass, by the length of the firing, and by the chemical quality of the furnace, as well as by the nature of the dust or vapor applied.

Although the "accidents" provoked by organic dusts may endow the glass with a superficial appearance of such fabrics as crepe and tulle, or even of snow, mist, and rain, the glass reveals its essential quality when patination has been used in combination with *marqueterie,* which was often the case in Gallé's work (Plates 113, 139, 188). Still more interesting results were possible when the patina was effected between two layers of glass (Plate 186a). The patinated glass could, moreover, be crackled, engraved, decorated "cold," or covered with layers of crystal. A detail of *The Carnivores* makes clear, in the midst of metallic foil bursting through two layers of glass, the tactile relief produced in the flower petals by patination (Plate 95).

Marqueterie de Verre Another process born of the new expressive needs was *marqueterie de verre*—"glass marquetry." After some hesitant experiments begun around 1889, Gallé felt ready in 1898 to write his friend Victor Chapier and tell him officially about recent developments in glassmaking techniques—patination and marquetry.

For *marqueterie de verre,* Gallé adapted procedures traditional in wood marquetry or mosaic and began to attach directly to the soft, hot material one or more sheet-thin pieces of colored glass of predetermined shape. Joining the fragments, or laminations, side by side, or superimposing them, he worked out a design already prepared in advance. In this way he could act like a painter and embellish the glass with every conceivable hue and tone. The potential seemed limitless.

Already in ancient times, glassmakers knew how to insert glass threads, bosses, lozenges, or cabochons into the hot vitreous mass. Then there were the Venetians who since the Renaissance had been sandwiching designs between two layers of glass. Jules Henrivaux even tells us that "in industrial crystalworks it was usual to include *millefiori* and refractor castings in crystal paperweights." It became Gallé's mission to push the process to its limits, and with his laminations placed in a "precise order, like pieces of stained glass," he succeeded, perhaps better than anywhere else, in expressing his dreams and designs. Frequently the *marqueterie* is encased with a layer of clear glass.

Many pieces that Gallé intended for *marqueterie* are in fact labeled *Etude* ("Study"), which means that, following an accident in firing, they were left in their first state.*

*To Gallé, the vases he marked *Etude* were what a sketch is to a painter—the first surge of inspiration, reduced by an accident to the state of a rough draft. But even in these pieces the artist's sensibility is revealed, and, though unfinished, they are very moving and much sought by collectors.

Even though the marquetry process offers multiple decorative possibilities, it also poses many difficulties (Plate 192). The glassmaker must, for instance, choose laminations whose coefficient of expansion is very close to that of the base piece—or risk breaking it. Furthermore, the glass must be reheated as many times as there are laminations to be added—and Gallé sometimes added several dozen. Then, with each new firing the problems and liabilities are compounded.

For a vase that has survived all the technical hazards, the final stage of its creation consists in using wheel engraving to reveal the submerged decoration, followed by trimming, polishing, and retouching. Glassmakers who adopt the *marqueterie* technique cease to be mere technicians and become painters. They enjoy an hitherto unknown freedom to vary at will the decorative and chromatic effects of their pieces (Plates 186b, 187). Moreover, the superimposition of layers greatly intensifies the colors, causing the glass to vibrate in an unparalleled way.

Marqueterie de verre allowed Gallé to translate all those much-loved themes inspired by his ardent observation of nature: a translucent landscape inserted in a bowl, where the four essential elements—sky, water, fire, and earth—are evoked in abstract lines (Plate 194); a jellyfish with a veritable fringe of tentacles (Plate 191); symbolic flowers, such as the one enveloped and incorporated into a bud vase (Plate 193); or the shimmer from a thousand fires, kindled by the incorporation of silver foil. In all such creations, as in many other, equally fascinating ones, the glass seems to live and breathe so as to give delight (Plates 70, 97, 98, 112–114, 126, 127, 129).

Abstract of the descriptive statement deposited by Gallé in support of his request for a fifteen-year patent protecting a type of decorative process called Patine sur cristal ou sur verre *("patina on crystal or glass")*

In the fabrication of glass or crystal, it often happens that the surface of the material is altered, disturbed, or contaminated while being worked in a paste state, the effect caused by exposure at this time to dusts from wood or coal combustion, and occurring by means of the working tools or the working hole in the kiln. In the glass industry such deposits of dust are considered to be technical flaws known by such names as "bubbles," "grease," "stitches," "mousse," etc. Concerned about such defects, I had the idea of using them as a decorative means, which permitted me, by inducing the effect in various ways, to obtain an entirely new type of decoration, called *patina*, the subject of the present patent application.

The dusts or ashes coming from the kiln, or the particles artificially produced or collected, deposited on the working tools, and then imbedded in the vitreous mass spread uniformly over the surface of the paste material, disturb, roughen, and then tear it in the working, and so modify the surface that it comes to look like fabric, crepe, or a thick cobweb, and to the touch can seem to be either coarse or fine. It is this mat texture that I call *patine du verre*, whatever the material employed for dusting the hot glass.

Such patination can occur on the exposed surface, or under a layer of crystal if the piece is blown, the bed of dust becoming imprisoned and compressed between two layers of glass. Unable to escape, the gas remaining from the original combustion presses against the glass paste and forms bubbles that lodge near the center of the mass. In this patina one can make decorative reserves, either by protecting them while still hot or once cold by cutting into the patinated ground, which can be accomplished with any of the engraving techniques—hydrofluoric acid, sand blasting, wheel carving—all providing an infinite variety of design possibilities.

Too, while the vitreous mass remains in a paste state, it can be embedded with fragments of hot glass, the whole then encased under a layer of crystal, left plain or itself patinated.

As this would suggest and as explained in the patent application submitted today for a type of *marqueterie sur verre ou cristal* ["glass or crystal marquetry"], I have the possibility of combining *marqueterie* with patination, the subject of the present application.

As examples of all the glass or crystal combinations that lend themselves to patination, I attach to the application a series of samples for which I now provide descriptions. [Hereafter followed descriptions of all the samples submitted by Emile Gallé, also diagrams of the kiln appropriate for his invention—that is, a kiln designed to receive the dusts from burning pine through a working hole connected to the inner chamber. A bellows, located in the opening, allowed the duration of the exposure to be limited.]

4. For the execution of this patina, the new utilization of the kiln and apparatuses in ways appropriate to this original result, as has been indicated.

5. As new products, the objects and articles of glass or crystal invested with this patina, giving the effect of matness with the appearance of fabric, crepe, cobweb, with or without bubbles and "stiches," combined or not with a type of *marqueterie,* which is the subject of my patent application, made this same day, for blown hollowware, molded and shaped works, vases, cups, plate glass, imitation stone, enamels, etc.

Paris, April 26, 1898

Resumé:

By this patent I wish to protect the ownership and the exploitation of my decorative process called *patine sur cristal ou sur verre* ["crystal or glass patina"], and I claim the following as the essential and distinctive character of my invention:

1. The utilization of natural materials that dust the glass or crystal as the material is being worked, the dust transmitted either by the working tools, mainly the marver, or by the working hole in the kiln, where the dusting is aided by a bellows, if this exists, all for the purpose of forming on the glass surface a decorative mat texture that I designate by the term *patina.*

2. The artificial dusting of the glass or crystal with all sorts of particles so as to obtain the effect of patination in every degree of texture, type, appearance, and color.

3. The use of the patina on an exposed surface or with decorative reserves cut into the ground, by any of the engraving or other processes now in use, in the form of a design, with the whole susceptible to casing under a layer of crystal or glass, which itself can be patinated as desired.

below: 189. Emile Gallé. *Peau de cristal* ("Crystal Skin"), c. 1900, height 230 mm/9", private collection. In a vase titled by Gallé himself, a patina has endowed the material with the compact, densely textured quality of pumice stone.

right: 190. Emile Gallé. *Vase with aquatic decoration*, c. 1900, height 260 mm/10 1/8", private collection. Here Gallé juxtaposed two strongly contrasted parts and thus produced a technical tour de force. In his simulation of the iridescences of submarine depths, he also proved himself to be a true alchemist of glass, for he achieved the effect by the tricky process of mixing air bubbles into the molten mass, along with metallic pearls and hot foils of different materials. Finally, the sculptor Gallé adopted the wheel and by carving away the surface layer revealed seaweed and a crab stranded on the ocean floor.

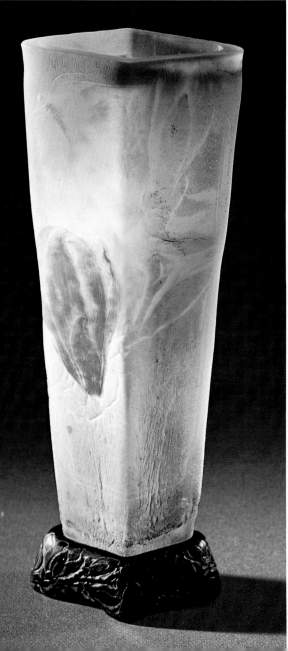

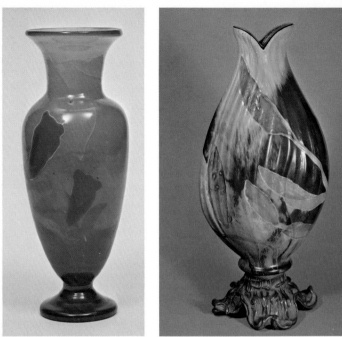

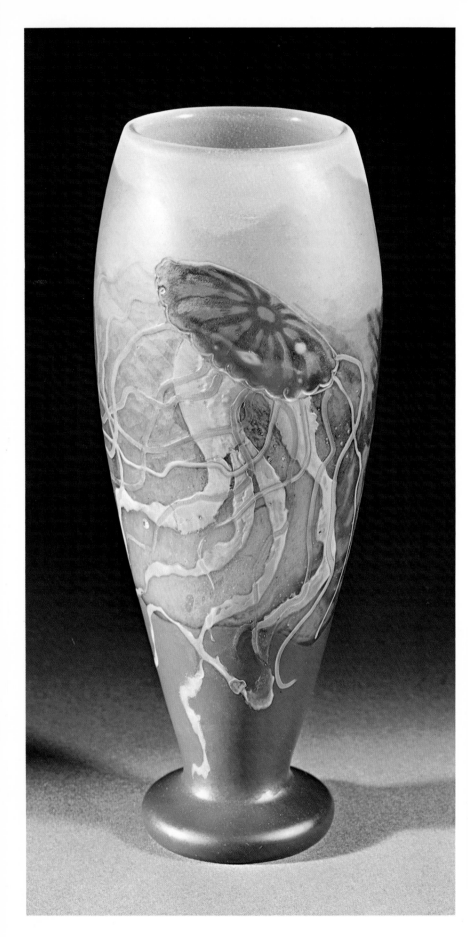

left: 191. Emile Gallé. *Vase with jellyfish*, c. 1900, height 260 mm/10 1/8″, J.-Cl. Brugnot, Paris. In this vase, created by an elaborate technique of *marqueterie* against a satin ground, the fascinating jellyfish with multiple tentacles painted red, orange, and indigo floats between two fathoms of water.

above left: 192. Emile Gallé. *Vase with floral decoration*, c. 1898, height 165 mm/6 1/2″, Musée du Verre, Charleroi. This piece shows the first stage of glass marquetry before the cutting wheel has revealed the decoration trapped in the lower layers.

above right: 193. Emile Gallé. *Vase with iris*, height 340 mm/ 13 3/8″, Musée de l'Ecole de Nancy. The shape of the piece echoes that of the iris bud it depicts. Signature on the bronze mount: "Gallé."

The plates on these two pages illustrate how Gallé signed his high-quality glass. **below left: 195.** *L'Amour chassant les papillons noirs* (Plate 93). **below: 196.** *Fiori oscuri* joins the signature on the base of a vase inspired by a verse from Robert de Montesquiou: *J'aime l'heure où tout changeant de forme/Le clair et l'obscur luttent ensemble* ("I love the hour when, with all forms changing/Light and shadow struggle together"). **right: 197.** *Le Sens de la Vie*, dedicated to the playwright Edmond Rostand. Collection J.-Cl. Brugnot, Paris. See Plate 73.

SOME CONTEMPORARY APPRECIATIONS OF EMILE GALLÉ

1878: "By combining engraving and enameling, and by borrowing some of the principles of Japanese art, Emile Gallé initiated a whole new evolution in glassmaking."

DIDRON, reporter on the Universal Exhibition

1886: "M. Gallé has known how to create an original art altogether his own. His works will remain as one of the most interesting examples of the glass industry."

EMILE GARNIER

1889: "Gallé already shows brilliantly just how much art, poetry, profound or exquisite intentions, delicate and rare thoughts can be put into the composition of a simple flower vase or a glass cup. It seems that matter could not be animated with more sentiment and spirit."

JULES HENRIVAUX

1899: "Thanks to Gallé, a refined and sublime material can convey quietude in one instance, in another a subtle sadness, and on yet a different occasion the poignant enigma of nature. In his combination of forms and shades, Gallé has captured all that the universe breathes of tenderness and all that this tenderness inspires in the soul that experiences it."

LA LORRAINE ARTISTE

1900: "His innovations opened hitherto unknown paths and taught a great lesson—nature's example is useful to industries that need inventions." "Here is a man who makes a passion for art understandable, as Vasari has described it among the Florentine masters; he gave plants a personality and a language; he rediscovered the mysterious laws of their being, whether enshrining their images in the marquetry of his furniture, or throwing them into his crystal pastes."

VICOMTE DE VOGÜÉ

Gallé's competitor Legras, director of the Verrerie de Pantin, gave this interesting opinion: "M. Gallé's manufacture, although small in volume, is interesting in its variety. It is true art glass—poetic, dreamlike glass—all that one would wish to exclude from commercial glassmaking. Most of his pieces with very original shapes are made with several successive layers of more or less colored glass. By attacking the material with hydrofluoric acid, and then with the wheel, the artist-engraver produces transparent depths and curious effects of light. M Gallé is the Meissonier or the Carolus-Duran of glassmaking."

1911: "The boldness of his life and character shine through his work."

ROGER MARX

". . . The multiple suggestions that arise from these enigmatic and 'speaking' vases—like a mysterious water noiselessly flowing from a secluded fountain."

LOUIS DE FOURCAUD

"It seemed as though the art of glass could go no further. An artist like Gallé makes us think of a quintessential abstraction that attempts to materialize the impalpable and to turn the dream into glass."

JULES HENRIVAUX

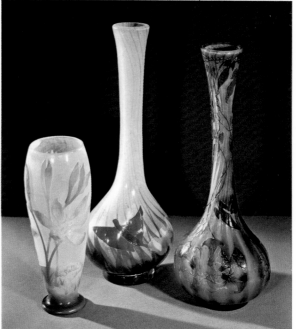

LES FRÈRES DAUM

Since he was a notary, it hardly seemed likely that Jean Daum (1825–85), father of Auguste and Antonin, would one day become the proprietor of a glassworks in Nancy. Established at Bitche since 1851, Jean Daum did have many Meisenthal glassworkers among his clients, but this did not automatically assure him a knowledge of their art. Then came the Franco-Prussian War of 1870, which resulted in first the destruction and then the annexation of Bitche by Germany, and ultimately the complete disruption of Jean Daum's life. With his family, he took refuge at Sarralhe in the Moselle before moving on to Dombasle and finally, in 1876, to Nancy. In 1878 circumstances combined to place him at the head of a factory for watch and tableware glass, founded in Nancy in 1875 by the glassmakers Avril and Bertrand.

left: **202.** Les Frères Daum. (a) *Pitcher decorated with enameled flowers*, c. 1900, height 250 mm/9 3/4"; (b) *Vase with columbines*, in a silver mount by Guerchet, c. 1897, height 140 mm/5 1/2"; (c) *Vase with autumn crocuses*, after a maquette by Louis Fuchs, c. 1900, height 180 mm/7". Musée des Arts Décoratifs, Paris.

right: **203.** Les Frères Daum. *Vase with dahlias*, 1896, height 150 mm/ 6", collection Daum, Nancy. Inscribed with thanks expressed by Antonin Daum to *mon meilleur ami* ("my best friend")—his brother Auguste—who brought new life to the Daum firm.

A neophyte in glass, Jean Daum needed a technical collaborator, and he found one in Marquot, the former director of a glassworks in the north of France. Daum then decided to continue the watch-glass manufacture, which enterprise survived until 1928, but to concentrate on developing tableware. Still, there were difficulties, and despite his goodwill and excellent qualities, Jean Daum could not overcome them all. Thus, he called upon his son, Auguste, to come in and improve what had stubbornly remained a faltering business.

Auguste Daum was born at Bitche in 1853, and, like his father, he did not belong to the glass trade, preferring instead to enter the legal profession. After graduation in law, he became clerk to the notary in Nancy. But in 1879 Auguste was forced to give up this line of development and to enter the family business.

To prepare himself for his new career, Auguste Daum began immediately to study the various processes of glass manufacture. He became a good administrator and gradually succeeded in improving the business. Then, in 1887, when the manufacturing position had been assured, Auguste's brother Antonin entered the factory, bringing it a new strength.

From this time forward, two essential characteristics came to prevail in the Daum operation: the family solidarity and self-confidence, and their excellent management, where nothing was left to chance. Antonin Daum (1864–1931) had graduated from the Ecole Centrale with an engineering diploma. Together the two brothers ran the glassworks in a spirit of great mutual respect, as can be seen in a vase dedicated by Antonin Daum to his "best friend," and brother, Auguste (Plate 203).

right: 204. Les Frères Daum. (a) *Vase in the form of a thistle*, 1900, height 440 mm/171/8"; (b) *Vase in the form of a rose*, 1900, height 330 mm/13". Collection Daum, Nancy. In both pieces, theme and form become one.

far right: 205. Les Frères Daum. (a) *Vase with enameled insects*, 1900, height 400 mm/15 5/8"; (b) *Vase with wading birds*, 1900, height 220 mm/8 5/8". Collection Daum, Nancy. In (a) the rising sun brings out the color and transparency of insect wings. In both pieces the influence of Japan is obvious, but the shapes are characteristic of Daum.

below: 206. Les Frères Daum. *Autumn Crocuses in Violet Mourning*, 1893, height 470 mm/18 1/2", Musée d'Art Moderne, Paris. The Daums made their reputation with a new style, here demonstrated in a long-necked bottle with an acid-etched naturalist decoration.

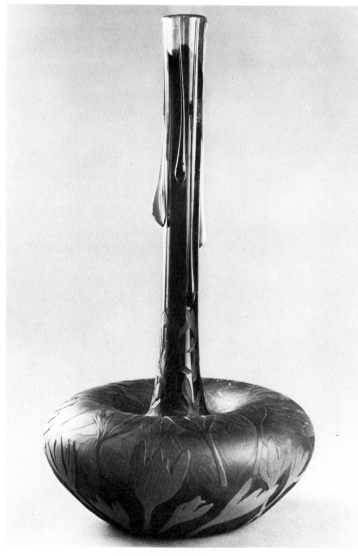

While Auguste undertook the house's commercial and financial direction, Antonin concentrated entirely on production, soon in fact learning to follow the most advanced trends in the decorative arts. Perhaps stimulated by Emile Gallé's success at the 1889 Universal Exhibition, the Daums opened a decorating studio. This was the beginning of an artistic output parallel to the production of glass tableware, with the result that the brothers issued pieces with both artistic and utilitarian qualities that brought their firm a special prestige (Plate 209).

By then the Daum installation had twelve crucibles, two furnaces, and a payroll of three hundred workers. The decorating studio alone engaged the energies of fifty people. Beginning in 1893, the Daums took part in all the great exhibitions, and already at the first one, in Chicago, they were classified *Hors Concours*. Among the pieces shown there was a vase entitled *Autumn Crocuses in Violet Mourning* (Plate 206). Dating from 1893, this work contains the germ of qualities that would ensure the Daums' future fame—the roughed-out shape, with its elongated neck, and the stylized naturalism of the acid-etched decoration. But even now the Daum brothers had won an international reputation.

Once the decorating studio began to function, Daum production evolved rapidly. Objects lost practical importance but gained in artistic value. By 1900 Daum had found its own style, a compound of nature and the precepts of Art Nouveau. The numerous pieces they presented at the Universal Exhibition aroused great enthusiasm in the public and moved one reporter, Louis Enault, to comment on "the high quality of these artistic

left: 207. Les Frères Daum. *Four "berluze" vases,* c. 1895, 1898, 1900, and 1918, collection Daum, Nancy. Although interpreted differently according to their dates, these pieces all faithfully represent the Daum style.

right: 208. Les Frères Daum. *Vase with crocus,* 1900, height 180 mm/7″, collection Daum, Nancy. This vase with stylized decoration launched a new lozenge shape, which Daum repeated c. 1925.

below: 209. Les Frères Daum. *Tumbler and jugs decorated with thistles and umbles,* before 1892, collection Daum, Nancy. Daum tried out new naturalist themes on glassware even before the decorating studio was opened.

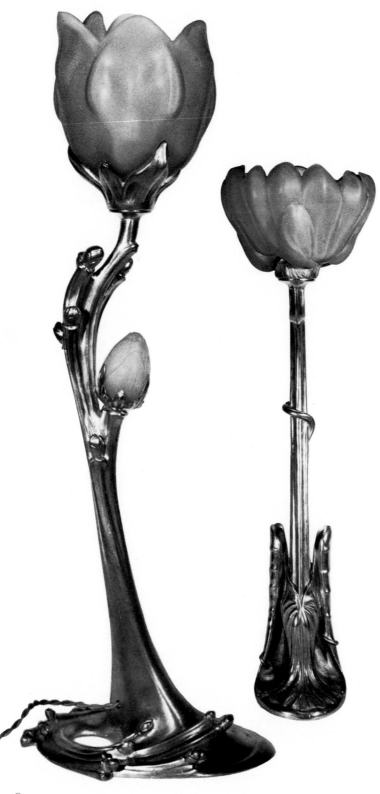

creations." The decoration, although inspired by nature, was liberated from all conventional restraints and stylized into abstract, even surrealist, designs (Plate 202). In perfect harmony with the ornament were the shapes, which in turn lost their rigidity, becoming undulating and movemented, metamorphosing into a svelte rose, a sharp thistle, or, later, an opulent gourd (Plates 204, 242). An almost baroque Art Nouveau, such pieces represented a new mode of poetic expression (Plate 239), comparable to Gallé's, in which the motif seems to be integral with the form, even to be confounded with it (Plate 229).

Along with these highly expressive pieces, 1900 saw the full blooming of simple, slender shapes, derived by Daum from 7th- and 8th-century Persian bottles—*les berluzes*, as the creators called them (Plate 207). At the same time, Daum also adopted globular, cylindrical, and lozenge forms (Plates 205, 208). Then, as a consequence of the Universal Exhibition, they put a brand new line into production—that of lamps (Plates 210, 211). For the first time, art glass appeared in combination with electric light, making its debut in the famous mushroom and flower lamps that created a sensation at the exhibition. Illuminated from within, the variable polychrome thicknesses of the vitreous material seemed to come alive and play back and forth across the glass forms. From the humble night lights to the great standard pieces and chandeliers, lamps became so important and successful that the Daums had to create new workshops for wrought-iron mounts.

The year 1900 also proved to be a climactic moment for technical advances, some of which became Daum specialities, such as wheel engraving, "hammering" (Plate 213),

left: 212. Les Frères Daum. *Vase with red poppy*, c. 1900, height 213 mm/ 8 1/2", private collection. Guided by the Impressionists, the artist has created a blurred decoration, obtained with the "intercalary" process.

below: 213. Les Frères Daum. *Vase with martagon lily*, 1900, height 190 mm/7 1/2", collection Daum, Nancy. The flower stands out boldly against a ground "hammered" with the wheel to make the surface look like faceted metal.

and the use of acid for "deep" cutting and a "frosted" effect (Plate 202bc). The Daums also took up intercalary and applied decoration (Plate 212); above all, they learned to get clever and seductive effects from the use of colored powders (Plate 242). The famous pâte-de-verre came from a later and different production, after being re-created in 1906 by Amalric Walter in the Daum studios. The pâte-de-verre works are true glass sculptures, in the form of cups, ashtrays, bookends, and statuettes (Plate 219).

Daum growth was indeed very great, and up to 1914 the well of the firm's inspiration seemed never to run dry. Then came the war and some months of interruption, but Daum managed to reopen in 1915 with a single furnace, manufacturing glass objects for hospitals and laboratories. After 1920 the Cristallerie Daum mainly issued pieces of simple shape with acid-etched decoration.

Except for glasses and tableware—trays, plates, flagons, jugs, bowls, and saltcellars—Daum pieces were never mass-produced. In a general way, the Verrerie de Nancy* undertook only those works that an artisan could fashion while hot or cold. The Daum brothers understood how to combine two great qualities: creative spirit and technical perfection. For this reason they take their place among those who elevated glass craftsmanship to the level of high art. To realize this, one has only to visit the Musée Privé des Cristalleries de Nancy, where the evolution of the business can be followed from its very inception.

*The Daum factory, the first factory to be established in Nancy, was known from the outset, and until World War II, as the "Verrerie de Nancy." This is how it was listed in the Didot-Bottin of that period.

THE DAUMS' COLLABORATORS

The Daums cannot be viewed apart from their collaborators, who were numerous, very talented, and important, a fact acknowledged by Antonin Daum. "What would I have become without you," he said to one associate in 1901, "I who cannot pass through the shed without burning my cape . . . nor, clumsy as I am, go into the decorating studio without sprinkling myself with bitumen or emery powder?"

As soon as he arrived, Antonin Daum began surrounding himself with a team of craftsmen and artists of great competence in every field—technical, chemical, and decorative—and worked to inspire them to enter into creative collaboration with one another. Among these participants, the first to be mentioned must be the master engravers Victor Marchand and Racadot, and then Eugène Damman, head of the decorating studio.

DUFOUR was another excellent artist, recruited from Badonvilliers, where he had made his first pieces as a decorator of faïence. Because of the crisis in faïence, Dufour, like many other craftsmen, turned to glass, since the technique of decorating with baked enamel is the same for both faïence and glass. He joined Daum in 1892, specializing in painted decoration, enameled in the manner of miniatures (Plate 246). With delicacy as his outstanding quality, he found inspiration in such classical sources as the *Fables* of La Fontaine, the landscapes of Pillement, traditional French *scenes champêtres*, and women in swings who seem to have come straight out of a painting by Fragonard. Although his works were very much appreciated among those who remained faithful to 18th-century taste,

214. Les Frères Daum. *Fructidor* ("September" in the calendar of the First French Republic), 1896, collection Daum, Nancy. In a design by Jacques Gruber, a decorator with Daum from 1894 to 1897, the fruit harvest is realized in a play of lines and silhouettes reminiscent of German Expressionist woodcuts. Signed in Gothic script.

215. Les Frères Daum. *Saltcellar and egg cups, decorated flowers and hens,* before 1900, collection Daum, Nancy. Motifs characteristic of the painter-decorator Dufour, who remained faithful to an 18th-century miniaturist style.

Dufour began just before 1900 to concentrate on floral decoration, doing so to take account of the new, developing taste for naturalism (Plate 215).

JACQUES GRUBER, a celebrated maker of stained-glass windows, entered the Daum firm as a glass decorator and remained there from 1894 to 1897. After learning to engrave, he created a series of highly artistic works, of which only eight to ten found a place in the regular repertory (Plate 214). For the most part, these were the vases inspired by the operas of Richard Wagner: *The Evening Star, Elsa's Dream* from *Lohrengrin*, and others based upon *Tristan and Isolde* (Plates 252, 253). Undoubtedly the source of the Wagnerian themes was Antonin Daum, a musician as well as a fervent admirer of Wagner. Later Jacques Gruber would earn fame for his beautiful stained-glass windows and cabinetmaking workshop.

EUGÈNE GALL, chief glassmaker and son of one of Antonin Daum's first collaborators, remained with the firm during the forty years of his career, from 1900 on. His pieces are unique and exceptional for the techniques that were successfully combined to create them (Plate 216). In Gall's glass can be found the shimmer and refinement of Impressionist tones. The forms are simple, yet powerful and vigorous—and also very personal. Some pieces, particularly those enhanced by a mount signed "Majorelle," are of an originality that borders on pure form, requiring little in the way of decorative elaboration (Plate 217).

HENRI BERGÉ was chief decorator, professor of drawing, and then director of the Ecole des Apprentis Décorateurs

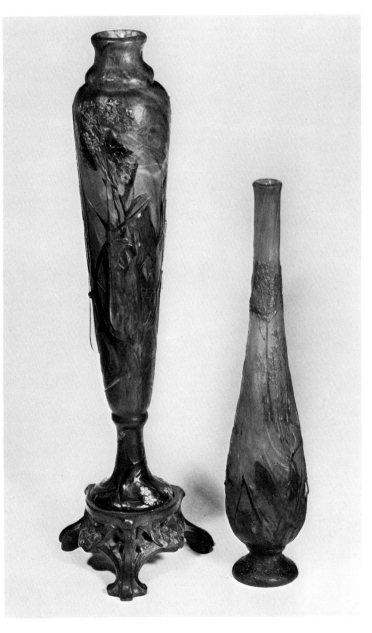

218. Henri Bergé. *Botanical watercolors made from nature*, private collection. In these models for vases executed under the direction of Bergé, Daum's chief decorator, flowers and leaves are studied in their smallest details.

219. Les Frères Daum. *Bat cup in pâte-de-verre*, length 170 mm/6 5/8″, collection Tamenaga, Japan. Signed by Amalric Walter, who made the work in the Daum studios.

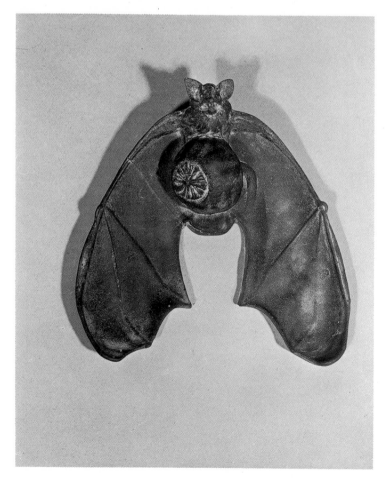

from 1900 to 1914. In fact, several study ateliers or "art laboratories" were opened at the Daum works, as well as an apprentice's school, where the projects and sketches from nature were completed. Primarily a painter and watercolorist, Bergé himself drew from nature, and his plates served as models (Plates 218, 235). Later he became a maker of maquettes, or three-dimensional models. His name is sometimes associated with that of Amalric Walter, creator of Daum's pâte-de-verre studio. For thirty years Henri Bergé remained a faithful and creative employee of Les Frères Daum.

AMALRIC WALTER, a graduate of the Ecole de Céramique de Sèvres, was perhaps the best-known member of Daum's creative staff, mainly because of his independent style and the special material he perfected—*pâte-de-verre* ("glass paste"). Called "ceramic paste" by journalists reviewing the 1909 Nancy exhibition, pâte-de-verre came about as a consequence of long research, after Henri Cros in 1884 had rediscovered what in fact was an ancient process. Beginning in 1906, Antonin Daum made an independent studio available to Walter. This became the generative source of stained-glass windows signed "Daum" and countersigned "Walter," as well as of many sculptural works, such as the *Loïe Fuller*, where long draperies became the pretext for a great, swirling play of Art Nouveau lines. The Walter atelier also produced cups, ashtrays, and trays decorated with such three-dimensional animals as fish, frogs, rabbits, etc. (Plates 219, 238). These pieces had great commercial success. Then, in 1919, Almaric Walter opened his own studio and began signing his name either alone or in association with Henri Bergé, who contributed naturalistic models. Easy to recognize, the works made by

220. Les Frères Daum. *Thistle Lamp*, 1900, height 455 mm/18″, collection Daum, Nancy. A major ironmaster, Louis Majorelle furnished Daum with lamp bases in wrought iron, marrying, as here, the strength of metal to the fragility of glass.

Walter are characteristic of an interesting oeuvre that was peculiar to Daum.

LOUIS MAJORELLE was a childhood friend of Antonin Daum. Together with Gallé and Daum, Majorelle remains one of the most typical and attractive figures of the Ecole de Nancy. Above all a master ironworker, he collaborated with the Daums from 1900 until World War I, providing them with lamp or cup bases in wrought iron, bronze, or even wood (Plates 210, 211). He loved to marry the fragility of glass to the tough durability of iron, a union in which one material reinforced the other. Majorelle made possible many cups in which the blown glass fills the free spaces of the metal armature. The most remarkable of Majorelle's works are the lamp mounts, where the harmony of shape and décor is enhanced by the delicacy of their execution (Plate 220). Louis Majorelle is also famous for the very fine furniture executed under his direction. But in iron mounts, Edgar Brandt is another name to remember, for he too made them for the Daums.

The Daum brothers always supported the personal initiatives of their collaborators. Thus, unlike Emile Gallé, who was his firm's only creator and innovator, the Daums assured the continuity and long life of their house. One contemporary critic noted: "The Daum studio is a model of artistic cooperation, for which there is no known prototype. Under the direction and stimulus of Antonin, the unique pieces of art were elaborated in a common effort by all the participants in the factory. It is surprising and without parallel to find painters, designers, acid and wheel engravers, technicians, chemists, and team leaders all collaborating in close and profound intercommunion, responding to the general inspiration. . . ."

DAUM TECHNIQUES

The Daum studios practiced all the known techniques, combining, contrasting, and perfecting them ceaselessly, but certain highly elaborate processes were peculiar to Daum. It is these that have been singled out for special study here.

Before 1890, the decorative techniques used by Daum included wheel and diamond-point engraving and the application of enamels to transparent and opaline glass, or to the glass of varying translucency that would become fashionable in the 1930s. But, above all, the Daum designers liked to concentrate on ornament with a gold base.

About 1891, after the example of Emile Gallé, the Daums began tentatively to use overlays of two and finally several layers of colored glass, exploiting the numerous possibilities for the transformation of the material by means of wheel and acid engraving. Moreover, they learned to include silver and gold foil between the glass layers, to imitate gemstones, and to employ both relief engraving and intaglio on the same piece.

But with the opening of the Daum decorating studio in 1891, a new adventure in glassmaking began. Everything was ready for a fresh departure, one in which technical originality would often be evident.

Daum's Intercalary Decoration

An especially delicate and elaborate process, intercalary decoration was studied in the Daum studios from their inception in 1891. By 1895 the most successful pieces—those ornamented with poppies or anemones or even the famous vase with trees in the rain—were beginning to appear (Plates 221, 222). Antonin Daum gave his description of intercalary decoration in 1901: "A form is decorated, engraved, or carved to various levels; it is then returned to the temperature suitable for the fusion of glass, after which it is cased with new layers of molten glass and fashioned into the definitive shape—bowl, cup, or vase. Finally, the wheel takes over, revealing, through the reserved foreground relief, motifs imprisoned in the lowest layers, integrating them with the general design, sometimes skimming lightly, sometimes plunging deep into the vaporous mass of vitreous material. . . . This process presents serious difficulties, and for the rare successes the glassblower must be given great credit."

In practical terms, the decorator preferred enamel painting on double- or triple-layered glass, encased in a new stratum of more or less translucent glass. By this means he could obtain pleasing effects of mystery and dream, accentuating them through the insertion of powdered colorants. The ground became blurred, unreal, and imprecise, and the decoration intimately mingled with it. But the definitive lines of the decoration would appear only after the last layers of glass had been blown. Now trees drip moisture, water moves—the decoration lives. Finally, wheel engraving on the surface of the glass lends an impression of deep perspective (Plate 212). The process can be seen in few examples, but it was one of the great decorative successes of the Daum firm.

Daum's Colored Powders

This technique offers many decorative possibilities, depending on whether the powdered colors are placed on the surface of or inserted between the glass layers. In the

221. Les Frères Daum. *Trees in the rain*, c. 1895–1900, height 280 mm/ 11″, collection Daum, Nancy. Intercalary decoration gives life to this product of a collaboration between decorator and glassmaker.

222. Les Frères Daum. *Vase with poppy*, c. 1900, height 130 mm/5″, collection Daum, Nancy. The intercalary method here permitted decoration with diffused tones, the imprecise, colored strokes lending the work a poetic quality.

left: **223.** Les Frères Daum. *Vases with spring and winter scenes,* c. 1910, height 112 mm/4½″ and 82 mm/3¼″, collection Daum, Nancy. Part of the *Quatre Saisons* ("Four Seasons") series, these pieces reflect the use of powdered colors inserted between two layers of glass and then enameled. This process, together with that of hydrofluoric acid, accentuated the perspectival effect.

below: **224.** Les Frères Daum. *Vases with peacock plumes,* c. 1910, height 102 mm/4″ and 230 mm/9″, collection Daum, Nancy. To represent the "peacock's eyes," strokes of deep-blue enamel were applied hot to the vitrified layer of blue-green powder.

second instance, crushed glass mixed with pigments is deposited on the marver and arranged according to a prepared design. The glowing paraison is then rolled over these powders, after which it is blown a second time and covered with a casing of glass. Vitreous material treated in this way appears speckled, like translucent precious stones, a similarity that becomes even more pronounced once the object has been struck by light. The Daums called their product *verre de jade* ("jade glass"), to show its resemblance to natural gems (Plates 240, 259). They used the technique from 1900 onward, just as electric light was entering more and more homes. A great many purely decorative vases also benefited from the ornamental effect of colored powders, used alone or as a ground for enameling. Thus, the vases in Plate 223 from *The Four Seasons* group contain pigments sandwiched between the glass layers, while the surface is enameled. In principle, "jade glass," once created, can be worked in many different techniques—with the cutting wheel or acid or with applied decoration (Plate 224). Highly valued, such pieces may be the most sensitive of all those produced by Daum, whose veiled decorations avoid all harsh contrast and thus assume the delicacy of an Impressionist canvas (Plate 225).

When the colored powders are not inserted between glass layers, but applied to the surface, the process is called "vitrification," after the terminology formulated by Daum early in the century. Fusion at the surface makes the powder adhere and become integral with the glass, endowing the surface with a rough appearance, which can be pronounced wherever the powder has accumulated (Plate 202a). Such "vitrified" vases acquired high artistic value

left: 225. Les Frères Daum. *Vase with floral decoration*, c. 1900, height 250mm/9 5/8″, collection Daum, Nancy. The flowers and leaves, applied hot, stand out from a ground of "jade glass." Like Gallé, although less boldly, the Daums adopted a naturalist décor of undulating lines drawn out over an attenuated form.

below: 226. Les Frères Daum. *Vases with insects on leaves*, c. 1900–10, height 250 mm/9 3/4″ and 221 mm/18 3/4″, collection Daum, Nancy. The insects, made of cabochons applied to a vitrified ground, reflect the period's naturalist tendencies.

once they were enhanced with applied decorations in the form of drops, cabochons, tears, insects, etc. Further enrichment could be obtained as acid etching was used to reveal a decoration within the mass (Plate 226).

True glass sculptures shaped like a wild watermelon, a tomato, etc., take on a special brilliance through the judicious use of vitrification (Plate 242). In principle, it can be said that this surface technique, together with that of inserted colored powders, is one of the most original processes employed by the Verreries de Nancy.

Daum's Wheel Engraving and "Hammering"

Although wheel engraving is a very ancient method of decorating glass, the Daums knew how to exploit it in novel ways and with special effects. Wheels of different sizes were used to abrade the fairly thick wall of the glass, most often in graduated cuts. By this means the engraver made the material look "hammered," as if it were metal, while also achieving an appearance of perspective and relief, especially where illumination plays or is trapped, creating zones of light and dark (Plates 213, 227).

Wheel engraving demands both time and talent; thus, it is not suitable for mass production. In his account of the 1909 exhibition, Antonin Daum expressed it thus: "The wheel engraver makes a personal work. He brightens or tones down as he wishes. Wheels of iron, copper, lead, wood, or cork give the glass a delicacy as caressing to the touch as to the eyes."

Sometimes hammering served to complete the acid etching, where the decoration required more precision

left: 227. Les Frères Daum. (a) *Vase with lily-of-the-valley*, c. 1894, height 122 mm/4 3/4"; (b) *Vase with anemone*, c. 1894, height 185 mm/7 1/4". Collection Daum, Nancy. Early applications of wheel engraving for a "hammered" effect. Later the opalescent ground would become opaque by virtue of accumulated layers of variously colored glass.

below: 228. Les Frères Daum. *Detail of Plate 204.* The circular facets of the "hammered" passages are readily distinguishable from those attacked with acid.

right: 229. Les Frères Daum. *Pine Cone*, c. 1900, height 240 mm/9 1/2", collection Daum, Nancy. Designed by the sculptor Bussières, this unique, deeply wheel-carved piece anticipated the Art Deco style of 1925–30. Daum's vases inspired by Bussières, such as *Leaping Carp, Singing Duck*, etc., are more sculptural than vaselike.

far right: 230. Les Frères Daum. *Vase with morning glory*, c. 1900, height 240 mm/9 1/2", collection Daum, Nancy. A rare work from a mold-blown series of vases so completely reworked with the cutting wheel as to belie the mechanical method used for forming the pieces.

and realism, or to obtain greater detail in areas beyond the reach of acid (Plate 228). The possibilities were endless.

Daum's Mold-blown Glass

For the most part, the Daums preferred a purely craft rather than a mechanical production. Occasionally, however, for the sake of technological experimentation, they turned to the machine and used it in their interesting and characteristic way. For instance, they took up the technique of forming glass by blowing the molten gather into a refractory, or fireclay, mold. Consisting of two parts held together by hinges, the mold left its mark on the pieces blown into it.

With their flower and landscape decorations, the forms produced in this way are well within the free, naturalistic spirit of the age. Still, a certain amount of stylization was essential, since the mold precluded elaborate details. In order to diminish, or even to hide, the "molded" look, the Daums often used the cutting wheel to retouch these vases. Thus, the pieces came out as quite personal works (Plates 230, 243).

When Lalique reintroduced mold-blown glass and began to practice it systematically, the company managed to save time and produce cheaper works while also preserving a certain artistic cachet.

Daum's Applied Decoration

Used alone or in combination with other techniques, applied decoration was also part of the individualized output of the Daum firm, and thus merits separate consideration.

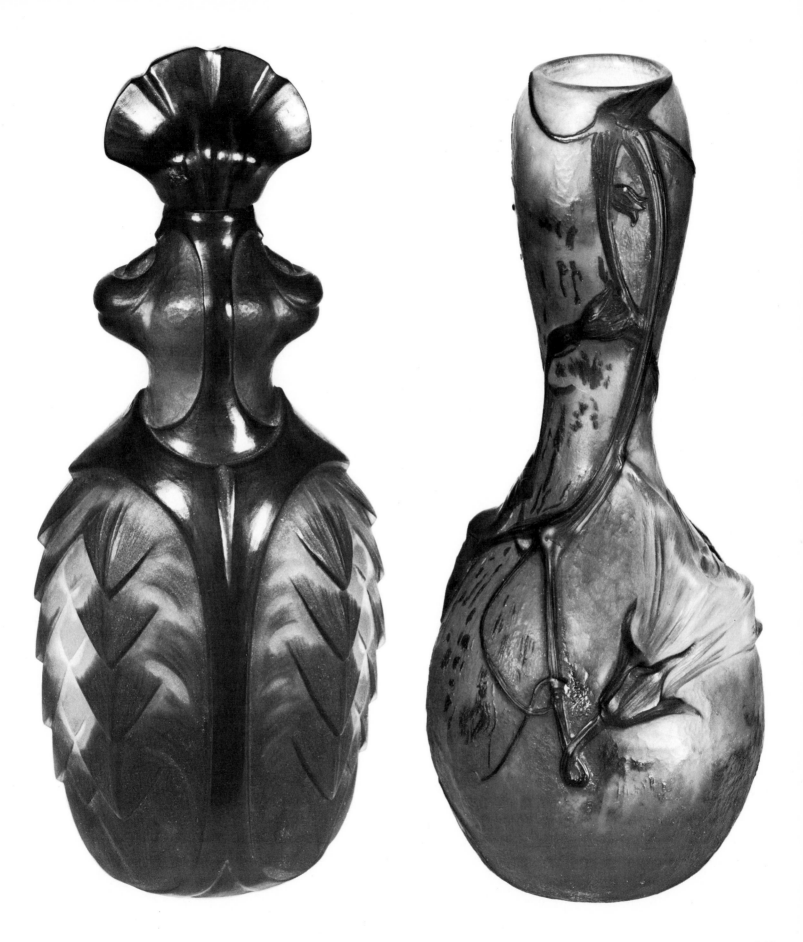

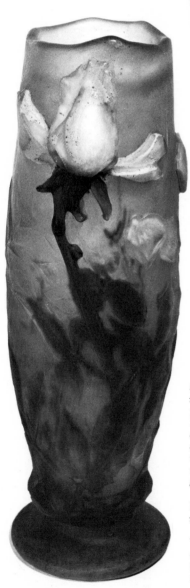

above: 231. Les Frères Daum. *Vase with pansies*, c. 1900, height 250 mm/9 5/8″, collection Daum, Nancy. The process used in this exceptional piece, completely encrusted with deep-applied decorations reworked with the cutting wheel, resembles Gallé's *marqueterie de verre*.

left: 232. Les Frères Daum. *Vase with rose*, c. 1900, height 310 mm/ 12 1/8″, collection Daum, Nancy. The rose and petals consist of colored glass laminations welded hot to the surface of the paraison, then reengraved with the cutting wheel.

Applied decoration can be realized in either high or low relief. If the former is desired, the decorator welds a hot fragment to a paraison, and adherence occurs the moment the weld has cooled. But owing to differences in the coefficient of expansion and contraction between the application and the host, the risks of cracking are very great.

The Daum decorator then worked the composite piece to its final state, just as he would have the various layers in cased glass. But since the effect of plasticity and polychromed mass could be obtained without overall layering, the process proved appealing for the lightness of the works that resulted.

The real craft in applied decoration lies in placing the laminations, or applications, so that after the piece has been reblown, prior to engraving, the decoration will have the distribution required for the work's intended shape and volume. A splendid success is the vase in Plate 232, where the petals and stem of a rose represent many sequential applications in varying degrees of relief, in the midst of other applications of greater depth, all reworked and wheel-engraved with such scrupulous care that the rose seems to spring out of its bouquet.

The applied decorations, which were usually hot when welded, could be added to the still-glowing host by pressure. Sometimes the pressure made such a deep incrustation that the engraver had to search for and reveal the motif in the thickness of the glass wall before the surface of the decoration could be reworked (Plates 231, 244a). As a consequence, the process seems very close to Emile Gallé's *marqueterie de verre* (Plate 113). More than ever, the master glassmaker became an artist by perfecting an almost sculptural technique (Plates 241, 245).

left: 233. Les Frères Daum. *Vase with anemones*, before 1900, height 250 mm/9 5/8", collection Daum, Nancy. Its ground etched and striped with acid, a process helped by diamond-point streaking through the protective bitumen, with flowers carved by means of the cutting wheel, and with painted and gold-heightened details, this finely wrought piece was one of the first realized in Daum's engraving studio.

right: 234. Les Frères Daum. *Detail of the "mouse-ear" vase in Plate 217.* Clearly evident is the acid etching around the floral decoration, as well as the reworking with a cutting wheel.

below: 235. Les Frères Daum. *Vase with orchid*, before 1900, height 230 mm/9", collection Daum, Nancy. Accompanied by Henri Bergé's full-scale study, this vase has a white acid-frosted ground and a flower decoration engraved with the cutting wheel.

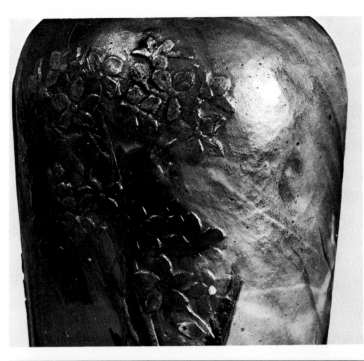

Daum's Acid Technique

In 1893 the Daum studios discovered the many decorative possibilities offered by hydrofluoric acid. Using it to enlarge their artistic scope, they made the acid method one of their specialities.

The Daum decorator took a brush loaded with Judean bitumen and painted his design on glass layered in different colors. He then plunged the piece into an acid bath, or attacked it with a brush soaked in the same liquid. This process had to be repeated several times before the motif, masked and therefore reserved by the bitumen, could be relieved in the several layers and colors. The work was finished when the piece had been washed in turpentine to remove all traces of bitumen (Plate 244b).

It must be stressed that decorating with acid is a delicate, sophisticated, and even dangerous undertaking. The 1893 vase entitled *Autumn Crocuses in Violet Mourning* was one of the first successes to be realized with the process (Plate 206). And the vases shown at the 1900 Universal Exhibition represent the culmination in this line of development, which can be seen in the pieces made by Eugène Gall (Plates 216, 217). Here the rich diversity of flowers and foliage was enhanced by means of a cutting wheel covered with emery powder (Plate 234), the procedure also followed for the orchid vase in Plate 235, created after a plate by Henri Bergé. In this work the ground was frosted—that is, treated with acid so as to alter the very nature of its surface. Moreover, the artist played freely with the composition, qualities, and thickness of the glass, as well as with the acid concentration and the length of the immersion in the hydrofluoric bath.

left: 236. Les Frères Daum. (a) *Enameled ca-rafe with cloisonné neck and stopper and a silver mount,* c. 1891; (b) *Soliflore Vase,* wheel-en-graved with a poppy, c. 1900, height 125 mm/ 5″. Collection, Daum, Nancy.

right: 237. Les Frères Daum. *Water bottle with sweet peas,* before 1900, height 335 mm/ 13 1/8″, collection A. Lesieutre, Paris. With a shape taken from Persian water bottles and a motif acid-etched on a frosted ground and enameled on the base, this piece possesses a perfect harmony of form and ornament.

A special effect was sometimes obtained by scoring the protective varnish with a diamond point (Plate 233). In some instances, the piece may be enameled on the surface, after which the frosted ground could be lightly hammered with the cutting wheel to make the piece more precious (Plates 236, 237).

The technical possibilities offered by hydrofluoric acid are numerous and varied, and some of the works that Daum created with it must be considered high art. One such piece is the vase inscribed "for my best friend" (Plate 203), and the detail reproduced in Plate 228 discloses large areas bitten by acid, which were then made expressive by supplementary work with the wheel, traces of which can be seen.

Daum and Pâte-de-Verre

It was in 1906 that Amalric Walter, while at Daum, took up the ancient technique of pâte-de-verre, which had been revived around 1884 by the sculptor-glassmaker, Henri Cros (Plates 268–274). Antonin Daum gave his definition of the technique some 24 years later when making his report to the jury of the 1925 Exposition des Arts Décoratifs: "Glass crushed into powders of different colors is mixed with a liquid binder to form a paste, which is brushed or stamped onto the interior relief surface of a fireclay mold formed upon a wax model. The pâte-de-verre shell is then covered, according to the thicknesses desired, with additional layers of vitreous paste. After drying, it is placed, either in its mold or bare as with soft procelain, inside the muffle furnace for the re-fusion of the glass. After firing,

the mold, which has become friable, falls to dust, allowing the piece to reappear with its colors, solidity, homogeneity, and details all scrupulously conforming to the model. It then has only to be cleaned and polished as desired."

This technique, in some ways, resembles the lost-wax process of casting bronze, where the wax melts away and thus can be used only once. In glass it produces an opaque material, close to a ceramic paste, but with a "bubbled" surface that is rough to both touch and sight. It brought out Amalric Walter's special talent, which can be seen in numerous pieces characterized by lively, warm, artistically shaded colors (Plates 219, 238).

238. Les Frères Daum. *Ashtray with field mouse,* after 1906, diameter 210 mm/8 1/4″, collection Tamenaga, Japan. Made in pâte-de-verre by Amalric Walter.

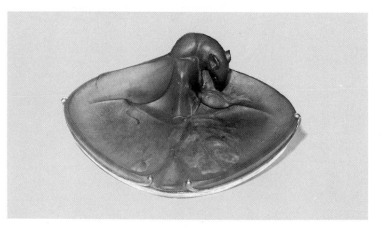

right: 239. Les Frères Daum. *Bowl with butterflies*, 1900, height 210 mm/ 8 1/4″, Musée de l'Ecole de Nancy. The lively shape and the colored applications formed like fantastic butterflies make this piece a highly baroque, poetic work.

below: 240. Les Frères Daum. *Cups with cicadas*, c. 1900, height 150 mm/ 6″ and 190 mm/7 1/2″, collection Daum, Nancy. Applied hot, the very beautiful cicadas on a "jade" ground evince the great skill of Daum's technicians.

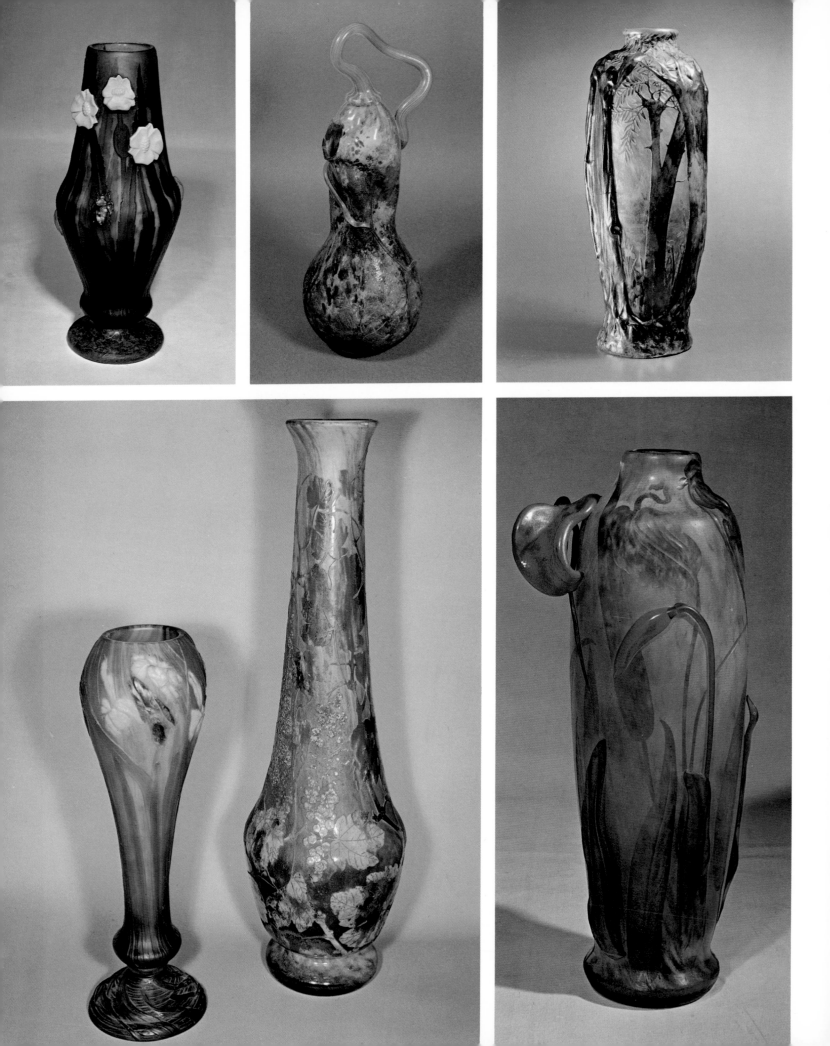

far left: **241.** Les Frères Daum. *Vase with buttercups*, c. 1906, height 390 mm/7 1/2″, collection J.-Cl. Brugnot, Paris. Wheel-carved thick foliage with applied flowers and gold-leaf insects.

left center, **242.** Les Frères Daum. *Gourd-shaped vase*, c. 1905–10, height 300 mm/11 3/4″, Musée des Arts Décoratifs, Paris. Powders of different colors were incorporated into the vitreous mass.

left: **243.** Les Frères Daum. *Vase decorated with a landscape*, c. 1905–07, height 292 mm/11 1/2″, Kunstmuseum, Coll. Hentrich, Düsseldorf. Mold blowing produced the illusion of deep relief, while acid etching and wheel carving completed the décor.

below far left: **244.** Les Frères Daum. (a) *Vase with floral decoration*, c. 1900, height 310 mm/12 1/8″. Several layers, some of them applied, were wheel-carved, producing in the base a simulation of foliage twisted around a bulb. (b) *Vase with plane-tree leaves*, 1903, height 450 mm/17 3/4″. Here, in a single piece, are displayed several different techniques: acid etching, a "jaded" ground, and wheel carving. Musée des Arts Décoratifs, Paris.

below left: **245.** Les Frères Daum. *Vase with exotic flowers*, c. 1900, height 390 mm/15 1/2″, collection J.-Cl. Brugnot, Paris.

DAUM'S SOURCES

Like Gallé, the Daum brothers were humanists of large, open spirit who took their inspiration from many sources and cleverly used them to create highly personal works. At first, they allowed their shapes and decorations to be influenced by regional ceramics and by 18th-century glassware (Plate 215), of which Nancy could boast many examples. The production reflected the taste of Daum's bourgeois clientele, who happily bought services decorated with small flowers, garlands, palmettes, or interlacements, all styled more or less after the famous wrought-iron grille-work of Nancy's Place Stanislas. The decorations were in black or bistre grisaille, or indeed in polychrome enamel. Daum's decorators of this period also favored scenes illustrating the *Fables* of La Fontaine, or the fashionable pastoral scenes after the manner of Fragonard or Pillement (Plate 246). But the influence of Venice was also felt, especially in the form of applied collars or in small, winglike handles (Plates 248, 250).

The Daums, moreover, followed Gallé in imitating mosque lamps and in enameling decorations taken from the arabesque designs made fashionable by Joseph Brocard (Plate 247). The Near East gave them the additional example of new shapes, such as Iranian water bottles and vases with long necks, from which they made the *berluzes* that became so characteristic of their studios (Plate 207). To flat-patterned, organic themes as intricate as Persian miniatures, Daum here and there added some new decorative elements—flowers, the Cross of Lorraine, interlacements recalling the barbarian art of Celtic Europe, or the stylized dragonflies so favored by the nascent Art Nouveau (Plate 247). Then there was antiquity, an inexhausti-

246. Les Frères Daum. (a) *Perrette and the Milk Jug*, c. 1895, height 70 mm/2 3/4″; (b) *Saucer with a landscape*, c. 1895, diameter 70 mm/2 3/4″. Collection Daum, Nancy.

247. Les Frères Daum. (a) *Vase with dragonfly*, c. 1895, height 150 mm/6″; (b) *Vase enameled with foliated scrolls and arabesques*, 1894, height 200 mm/8″. Collection Daum, Nancy.

right: 248. Les Frères Daum. *Enameled vase with ca-bochons*, 1891, height 135 mm/5 1/4″, collection Daum, Nancy. Made soon after the opening of Daum's decorating studio, this piece is Islamic in both shape and ornament, but Venetian in the applied collar.

far right: 249. Les Frères Daum. *"Egyptian" vase*, c. 1897, height 165 mm/6 1/2″, collection Daum, Nancy. Displayed at the 1900 Universal Exhibition, this piece faithfully reflects Champollion's account of the frescoes discovered in the underground chambers of Beni-Hassan.

below: 250. Les Frères Daum. *Vase with peacock plumes*, c. 1895, height 270 mm/10 1/2″, collection Daum, Nancy. The curious shape derives from a 16th-century Spanish prototype.

ble resource for new forms and decorations, especially the frescoes of Beni-Hassan, which contemporary scholars mistakenly thought illustrated the glassmaker's art (Plate 249). But what these murals depicted were workers stoking the hearth fire for metal casting. The Daums seem also to have known Roman sculptures, which gave them models for nobly proportioned human images (Plate 214).

The influence of German music is evident in Symbolist themes that the Daums took from *Lohengrin* or *Tristan and Isolde* (Plates 252, 253). This is understandable, since Antonin Daum, an accomplished musician, shared with Gallé a great admiration for Richard Wagner. But the Daums were also very much attached to their adopted country and often paid tribute to the great moments in its history, doing so in a deliberately medieval style. René II, Lorraine's great maecenas Duke, is honored on a flask whose opposite side illustrates the Porte de la Craffe, one of Nancy's architectural treasures (Plate 251). Filled with the new ideas of the young Ecole de Nancy, of which they were cofounders with Emile Gallé, the Daums looked to nature for their real inspiration. Equipped with new or revived techniques, they found novel shapes and decorations in the world of plants and animals, as well as the poetic sentiments to make them expressive (Plate 257). Antonin Daum even gave his name to a new variety of begonia, discovered in 1880 by the celebrated Nancy horticulturist, Victor Lemoine. Then came new objects, reflecting literature through the use of brief quotations (Plate 258).

Beginning in 1900, naturalist decoration dominated the Daum studios, and this could be found in glassware as well as in the most elaborate pieces (Plates 255, 256). But also to be felt in their work was the influence of Japan, to whose

right: 251. Les Frères Daum. *Flask with an equestrian portrait of René II, Duc de Lorraine*, c. 1895, height 250 mm/9 7/8", collection Daum, Nancy. Symbolic of the Daums' patriotic attachment to their adopted country, and an expression of the contemporary taste for things medieval.

far right: 252. Les Frères Daum. *Elsa's Dream*, 1894, height 160 mm/6 1/3", collection Daum, Nancy. Inspired by Wagner's opera *Lohengrin*.

below: 253. Les Frères Daum. *Tristan and Isolde*, c. 1900, height 380 mm/15", collection Daum, Nancy.

Some examples of signatures found in Daum pieces

signatures à l'or: → 1890 peuvent se retrouver de 1903 à 1906

1890 à 1895 gravées à la roue

1895 à 1900

1900 à 1905

vers 1911   *1910 à 1915*

157

far left: 254. Les Frères Daum. *Vase with iris and frogs*, 1900, height 200 mm/8″, collection Daum, Nancy. Rushes and iris encourage an exercise in *japonisme*.

left: 255. Les Frères Daum. *Vase with magnolia*, 1900, height 490 mm/19 1/8″, private collection. As a leaf falls lightly from the flowering branch, aesthetic inspiration and poetic sentiment receive free expression.

below left: 256. Les Frères Daum. *Footed glasses*, collection Daum, Nancy. Together the two pieces suggest the stylistic evolution, from Neoclassicism to Ecole de Nancy naturalism, that occurred in Daum glassware.

lessons in reductive style the Daums responded along with all the other artists of the period (Plates 205, 254). Thanks to the Far East, Daum rediscovered the art of linear and spatial simplification, which left the field free for the poetic imagination. Stripping away everything superfluous, the Daum designers purified and freed their aesthetic (Plate 255).

Whatever their inspiration or sources, the Daums always remained faithful to one objective, that of enhancing the material. Antonin Daum articulated the policy in 1904: "Shapes and decorations are based upon this principle: durable and boldly painted, the motifs always come from a clear, vigorous idea, easy to appropriate, but above all captured by the richness of the material. Flowers, fruits, small beasts, and landscapes are used less for their graceful curves and symbolic attitudes than for their ability to underline the glowing, gemlike, reflective properties of that marvelous substance—glass" (Plate 259).

right above: 257. Les Frères Daum. *Bowl with fish, jellyfish, and starfish*, 1901, height 250 mm/9 5/8″, collection Daum, Nancy. Relief carving, harmoniously blended tones, dynamic, nautilus-shell form all contribute to a sense of poetry as well as of aquatic life.

right: 258. Les Frères Daum. *Vase with lily*, c. 1898, height 290 mm/11 1/2″, collection Daum, Nancy. Softly toned amphora inspired by a verse from Victor Hugo: *Ils rangent leur barque au port, leur vie à la sagesse* ("They steer their ship to port, their life to wisdom"), collection Daum, Nancy.

far right: 259. Les Frères Daum. *Vase with dragonfly and toad*, c. 1900, height 360 mm/14 1/8″, collection Daum, Nancy. Already treated by Emile Gallé in 1889, this theme served for one of Daum's most original and technically perfect works.

left: 260. Les Frères Muller. *Vase with floral decoration*, c. 1910, height 300 mm/ 11 3/4″. Made by Désiré Muller, using the *fluogravure* process, for the crystalworks of Val Saint-Lambert.

below: 261. Les Frères Muller. *Vase with bunches of grapes*, c. 1900–10, height 150 mm/6″, collection S. Deschamps, Paris. Wheel-engraved to reveal the decoration deep within the several layers of cased glass.

LES FRÈRES MULLER

Up to 1914 the Muller mark covers the work and common efforts of a whole family of artists and glassmakers, altogether nine brothers and one sister. They came originally from Kalhausen on the Moselle, near Saint-Louis, where the older brothers had been apprenticed to a glassmaker. Fleeing the German occupation that resulted from France's 1870 defeat, the Mullers settled at Lunéville, outside Nancy, in the French sector of Lorraine.

Where could the Mullers better exercise their trade than in the most prestigious firm of the region, that of Emile Gallé, then in full swing? Here indeed, around 1885–90, went the oldest brothers, Désiré and Eugène. Specialists in engraving and decorating, they would emerge as the most gifted and artistic members of the Muller clan. Three other brothers, Henri, Victor, and Pierre, entered Gallé's factory as apprentices and there learned the rudiments of their craft.

Under the influence of Henri, the most enterprising and commercially oriented of the group, the Mullers—all excellent artisans—decided to set up their own business. Around 1895–1900 they opened a decorating studio on the Rue Sainte-Anne in Lunéville, working with forms blown to their specifications by the Hinzelin glassworks near Nancy. A family business, it became even more so when the other brothers and their sister joined in the operation.

Each of the Mullers, according to ability, had his or her own responsibilities. Emile and Eugène both searched out and then drew models and motifs, but most frequently it was Emile, a highly skilled craftsman, who wheel-engraved the designs. Around 1900, a propitious period for new ideas and fresh departures, they experimented with every kind of decoration, including all the means of engraving—by wheel, by application, and, above all, by acid, which became a Muller speciality. The family learned to exploit the full range of effects that could be had from wheel carving and acid etching on vases cased or layered with many different colors (Plate 261). They could engrave vases built up to as many as seven layers—a remarkable achievement! As impressive in their control of tonal gradations as in their sense of design, they created works with the qualities of true painting, where the eye becomes lost in a kind of trompe-l'oeil. And as followers of Emile Gallé, they quite naturally observed the precepts of the Ecole de Nancy, stylizing flora and fauna in the free, broad, sketchy manner learned from the Far East (Plates 265, 266). Too, their favorite themes were insects, bats, butterflies, the leaves and bunches of grapes, chestnut foliage, iris, orchids, thistles, etc., all popular motifs frequently seen, especially in the creations of Gallé (Plate 267). So thoroughly did the disciples follow the lead of the master that the Mullers' work could, on occasion, be confused with that of Gallé himself, were it not for the signature. Sometimes they even underlined their ideas with a quotation, which made the piece a *verrerie parlante*. Thus, on the cornet vase in Plate 262 a verse from Victor Hugo mingles with the unfurling of creepers and reeds, the better to make us aware of "the splendid pond where swarms a whole mysterious world." The material itself—alternately impure, muddy, and lustered—adds to this impression, creating an ambience, a state of mind. The Mullers well knew how to use such an evocative substance, as can

262. Les Frères Muller. *Vase with aquatic plants*, c. 1900, height 260 mm/10 1/8″, Musée de l'Ecole de Nancy. The unfurling creepers, the tangle of reeds, and the variable impurities in the material express a verse from Victor Hugo: *l'étang splendide où pullule tout un monde mystérieux* ("the splendid pond where swarms a whole mysterious world"). Occasionally the Mullers followed Gallé and created a *verrerie parlante*, reinforcing their poetic intention with a line of verse.

263. Les Frères Muller. *Jug decorated with ladybirds on plane-tree leaves*, height 260 mm/10 1/8″, Musée de l'Ecole de Nancy. This piece, with its orange metallic reflections, rivals the most beautiful creations of the Ecole de Nancy.

right: 264. Les Frères Muller. *Lamp with owls and bays*, c. 1900–10, height 582 mm/23″, Musée de l'École de Nancy. The nocturnal animals, fixed in flight, endow this lamp with the mysterious and disquieting ambience of night.

be seen in the particularly interesting jug and lamp reproduced as Plates 263 and 264. On the one insects applied hot stand out from the orange, metallic-luster ground sprinkled with plane-tree leaves, while on the other, bats flutter in the sky, watched by an owl perched disquietingly upon a branch, as if, like all the other creatures, awaiting the proper moment to escape from its glass prison.

Only a few pieces from the Mullers' first production seem to have survived, since in their great exactitude, the creators destroyed all pieces that failed to meet expectations. But then it is possible that some of the house's works came out unsigned.

Around 1910 the crystalworks of Val-Saint-Lambert, near Liège in Belgium, invited Désiré Muller, the founder of the family business and its most accomplished technician, to help perfect a particular technique—*fluogravure* (Plate 260). This was a process designed to provide an attractive alternative to the enamel-dust injections practiced by Gallé and Daum. Combining enameling and engraving with acid, fluogravure reduced the risks posed by more elaborate techniques.* It required only that the glassmaker "cover or touch monochrome or cased glass (in two, three, or even four different color layers) with enamels of various tonalities, disposed according to the exigencies of the design and then fixed by subjecting the piece to the action of acid."

*Fluogravure created its own characteristic effects, according to R. Chambon in *Art verrier 1865–1925—Exposition de Bruxelles 1965.*

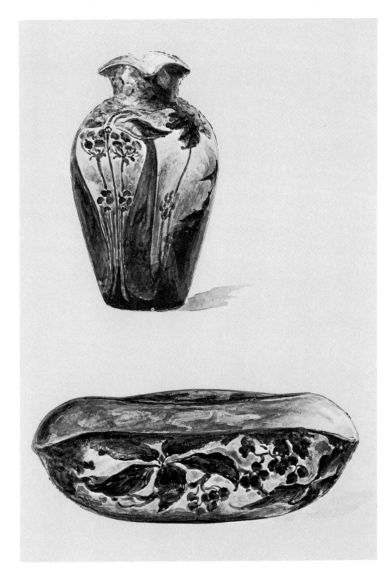

left (265) and above (266): Les Frères Muller. *Sheets of watercolors,* collection R. Chambon, Marcinelle. These stylized themes of flora and fauna, influenced by Japanese art, served as models for vases *à la manière de Daum.*

right: 267. Les Frères Muller. *Vase with bluets,* c. 1900–14, height 400 mm/15¾″, collection R. Chambon, Marcinelle. A decoration of highly stylized, naturalist forms has been cleverly designed in relation to the alternately swelling and tapering forms of the vase's shape.

At the same time, the other Mullers continued on at Lunéville, even moving to larger quarters in the Rue de la Barre, where they could exploit their now famous acid-etching process on a semi-industrial scale. But when the 1914 war broke out it not only cost the Mullers the life of Eugène, killed at the front; it also interrupted their business and scattered the entire clan. Emile found himself working as a wheel engraver at Choisy-le-Roi, and Jean, Auguste, and Camille in various capacities at Houdaille in Sèvres.

In 1919 the Mullers succeeded in buying back the Hinzelin factory at Croismare, while continuing to decorate glass in Lunéville. They now employed almost three hundred workers, thanks to their having developed an industrial capacity for the specialized manufacture of lamps and ceiling lights, using the technique of pigments incorporated between two layers of glass.

Without officially joining the Société de l'Ecole de Nancy, they followed its principles. Indeed, they obsessively sought mastery of their means, and thus took their place among the great glassmakers of the period, producing in their most original work objects of considerable artistic interest.

Up to 1914 the signature includes the words "Muller Croismare, près Nancy," engraved in diamond point or with the cutting wheel, or signed in gold. After 1919 they signed "Muller Frères Lunéville."

In 1936, as a result of the economic crisis, the Mullers could no longer survive, and, like many others, they found it necessary to close their doors. At the end of the decade the outbreak of World War II destroyed all hope of reviving Les Frères Muller.

above: 268. Henri Cros. *Mythological group in polychromed terra-cotta*, c. 1885, height 180 mm/7″, Musée du Petit Palais, Paris. Before executing a piece in pâte-de-verre, Cros sometimes made a model in terra-cotta.

left: 269. Henri Cros. *Circe*, 1891, height 930 mm/36 1/2″, Musée National de la Céramique, Sèvres. Among the important pâte-de-verre pieces in which Cros expressed himself freely, *Circe* symbolizes *l'Eternal féminin* ("Eternal Woman"), but a work of such immense scale also constitutes a technical triumph.

Pâte-de-Verre

Around 1880 certain of the more reflective and experimental artists had the idea of developing a fusible material that could be worked in either a paste or a liquid state. Moreover, this vitreous substance would, upon firing, become hard, translucent, and capable of being carved like sculpture, all the while that it offered the charm and appeal of nature's own colors.

Finally, it was Henri Cros who discovered, or rediscovered, a marvelous "new" material—*pâte-de-verre*—which in fact had already been known to the antique world and even described by Pliny in Book XXXVI of *Historia naturalis.* Jules Henrivaux tells us that "the ancients drew very pretty effects from glass and manipulated it in surprising ways. They were able to model it cold, like clay. Some of their glass has a special fragrance; some has the malleability of metals, so that when thrown on the ground, it bulges out of shape, but can, without risk of breaking, be straightened out with a hammer," thanks to the material's great porosity.

From the beginning the pâte-de-verre process seemed to invite secrecy and mystery, with the result that many legends and much mystery grew up around the kind of glass it produced. According to Petronius, the Emperor Tiberius was so concerned that the process not become generally known that he had a pâte-de-verre worker beheaded.

In our time the term is often used improperly to designate opaque glass, usually cased up to several layers, in which powdered-enamel colors have been incorporated during firing. But even when cased glass seems a close approximation of true pâte-de-verre, the difference in manufacture is great. So far as we know, Emile Gallé never made an object in pâte-de-verre. Yet the term is very frequently applied to his nontransparent, polychrome glass.

Pâte-de-verre is obtained by mixing, while cold, crushed glass, powdered enamels, and a binder, usually water. The paste thus formed is applied to the inner relief surface of a mold, after which the mold and its vitreous contents are fired, causing the elements of the pâte-de-verre to fuse and cohere. Once the mold is removed, if it has not crumbled in the kiln, the glass form stands free like a sculpture, fully colored in the mass.

After Cros, other great glassmakers took up pâte-de-verre and made it their preferred material: François Décorchemont, Albert Dammouse, Georges Despret, Ringel d'Illzach, and Amalric Walter (for Daum). As we shall see, each of them worked variants upon the pâte-de-verre technique.

HENRI CROS (1840–1907)

Henri Cros was born in Narbonne to a family of researchers and scholars in art, philosophy, and science. His father, a modest schoolteacher, tried to formulate a "theory of the intellectual and moral man." His eldest brother, Antoine, became a physician and, in his spare time, a poet. The author of *Décoordinations,* he also left behind a series of strange and symbolic watercolors. As for Charles, the youngest of the brothers, he was a professional poet and a part-time scholar who pioneered in both phonography and color photography. Charles, moreover, made his own attempt at inventing the automatic telegraph and telephone, presenting it at the 1867 Universal Exhibition.

Henri himself possessed the kind of creative imagination that quite naturally drew him to the plastic arts. Simultaneously a painter, a watercolorist, a sculptor, and a ceramist, he realized what may be his most important discoveries in the art of glassmaking, for it is to him that we owe the reconstitution of the ancient technique of pâte-de-verre.

At eleven years of age, Cros accompanied his parents when they went to live in Paris. It was also in the bosom of his family that Henri acquired his literary and artistic education, for among the Croses the love of antiquity and the cult of beauty constituted a tradition. Thus endowed with vast culture, Henri had the ability to read in classical literature and understand the explanations of lost techniques. But he also decided to become an artist, which prompted him around 1855–56 to enter the Ecole des Beaux-Arts, there studying under the painter-sculptor François Jouffroy and the sculptor Jules-Emmanuel Valadon. At the same time, Henri also joined the studio of

the classicizing painter Louis-Jules Etex, a former pupil of Ingres. Here he found a purity of line, a natural harmony in poses, and a distinctive color that accorded perfectly with his own aspirations. His personal feeling for beauty seemed at one with the Greek canon of the *Beau idéal*. In his art, however, Henri Cros made no attempt to render Greek and Roman art precisely as he found it. Rather, he simply evoked antiquity in a highly personal manner, doing so by integrating his sense of classical style with elements of "modernity" (Plates 268, 269).

From 1860 to 1865 Henri Cros worked as as a sculptor and executed several important pieces in marble, bronze, terra-cotta, and even alabaster. Often his subjects were his friends, parents, poets, fellow sculptors, and contemporary musicians, all of whom he represented with surprising naturalism. He also painted, executing many portraits and small mythological pictures. A scrupulous artist, Cros made numerous preparatory drawings in which, with a few strokes of the pencil, he could fix an attitude or a silhouette. Later, he never attempted a pâte-de-verre piece without first having made a pencil sketch, as can be seen in the many drawings preserved by the artist's collectors.

But with his inquiring mind and quick intelligence, Cros could not merely rest upon his early successes. He continued to study in the museums, always searching for new means of expression. Intrigued by the encaustic painting technique found in the Pompeiian frescoes owned by the Louvre, the young artist managed to recover the process from an antique text. He then began binding his colors with wax for portraits of his wife, children, and friends; also for a number of paintings based upon mythological themes. Having become very accomplished in this technique, Cros collaborated with the archivist Charles Henry to prepare and publish a well-documented, and much-applauded, essay entitled *L'Encaustique et autres procédés de peinture chez les Anciens—Technique et histoire*.

Painting with wax soon led Cros to use the material for modeling figures, at first in monochrome and then with tints of color. But since the highly soluble medium made it difficult to realize a perfect model, he decided to form clay molds from which to take plaster casts that he could then cover with wax colored precisely as he wished. Beginning in 1867, Cros exhibited wax figurines, mostly of historical or legendary subjects, among which could be found a *Charles VII* and an *Isabeau de Bavière* representing 15th-century, pre-Renaissance France. In 1873, from the same series, he exhibited *The Tournament Prize*, a magnificent composition of five figures clothed in fabrics rich—as Berenson might have said—in "tactile values." Mysterious in their reserve, as though fixed for all time by a magic wand, these personages seem the materializations of a dream, the symbols of waiting and solitude, themes so dear to those precursors of Art Nouveau—England's Pre-Raphaelites. Later, in his great pâte-de-verre compositions, he would return to this world of myth and suggestion.

Using the same medium, Cros went on to create contemporary figures, even though the very fragile wax fades, yellows, and generally deteriorates with time. Because of this problem he sought to ameliorate the inconveniences with a firmer, more durable material, but one with a similar appearance—tender and soft in coloring, delicate in grain, supple and semitransparent. Thus ori-

272. Henri Cros. *The Incantation*, dated June 1, 1891, height 310 mm/ 12 1/8″, Musée National de la Céramique, Sèvres. While this piece is in terra-cotta, a second version, dating from 1892, exists in pâte-de-verre. The purpose of the antique figures is to evoke poetic reveries of the past.

ented, Cros would have been fully prepared to respond to Pliny's explanations of the different methods of working glass—the *nobilis liquor*. He may also have found inspiration in the antique pâte-de-verre displayed at the Universal Exhibition of 1878, as well as in the examples that were to be seen in the Egyptian rooms at the Louvre. Cros' first attempts to reinvent a special and totally lost technique date from 1882. They proved laborious and difficult, involving the artist in every conceivable compound of fusible, vitreous elements, before finally he hit upon the ideal combination. He also had to study minerals and chemistry, and, like a new Bernard Palissy, he went so far as to construct a furnace with his own hands in his house on Rue de Regard. In 1907, immediately after Cros' death, Maurice Savreux wrote that the first modern pieces of pâte-de-verre—small medallions imitating antique cameos—were baked on the grill in the fireplace of the determined inventor's apartment.

Some financial help allowed Cros to open a studio in 1885, and to acquire a furnace of the size necessary for his research. However, the works he made at this time are variable in quality, their relief imprecise and the material full of bubbles and other imperfections. They are, above all, medallion-like masks of women with sweet and serene expressions—bacchantes, sirens, and blond nymphs— plus an Apollo standing out from a sun disk. The bust of a young girl in Plate 282 provides a good demonstration of Cros' initial desire to treat pâte-de-verre like a sculptural material.

These pieces, exhibited in 1889, won Cros a Gold Medal, and drew the attention of Henri Roujon, France's

Minister of Fine Arts. Thanks to Roujon, the Sèvres factory, hoping for its own renewal through young talent, gave Cros a studio and a kiln around 1892. This permitted the artist to continue his work without material care, and eventually to create at Sèvres his most ambitious and important works. Beginning in 1891, he took the risk of making his models larger, as in *Circe* at the Musée de Sèvres (Plate 269). What a technical feat this piece is! Drawn out to almost a meter, undulating and sensual, Greek via Ingres (does it not recall *La Source?*), it represents the art of Henri Cros at its most sumptuous and beautiful. The seductress enslaves the man, subjecting him to her fatal power, in the broadest sense of the term. Here is Eve the wondrous—Temptress and *l'Eternal Féminin*. Continuously self-renewing, the theme of the *femme fatale* recurred not only throughout the career of Henri Cros but also throughout the art of the entire era that he helped to create.

Probably from the same period is the plaque called *La Femme* ("The Woman"), in which the subject, her hair blowing in the wind, holds the reins of a team of sea horses, those favored creatures of the age's Symbolist bestiary (Plate 273). The whole scene, unlike *Circe* with its strongly contrasted tonalities, exhales a pearly evanescence, making it a triumph of the sort of delicacy possible in glass. One could well believe that Cros found himself so taken with the soft flesh tones of a Renoir *Bather* that he tried to render them in pâte-de-verre.

On the other hand, *The Incantation* (Plate 272), by its very title as much as by its expressive content, is a work of soothing lyricism. Because it was first made in terra-cotta, this relief also provides a good demonstration of the actual difficulties posed by pâte-de-verre, a material that only reluctantly yields touches and details that are readily obtainable in clay. Of course, Cros could very well have wanted to create a suggestive rather than a precise impression of the original lines, and by this means to challenge the imagination and induce reverie.

These one- and two-figure works were the prelude to the great decorative compositions that Cros would make from 1892 onward. One of them, *The History of Water*, is a wall fountain executed for the entrance to the Musée du Luxembourg. In 1900 came *The History of Fire*, which won a Gold Medal at the Universal Exhibition. "A remarkable work," said Henrivaux. For the Water and Fire allegories, Cros probably owed a debt to Pompeiian frescoes, with their qualities comparable to those that the artist loved in Puvis de Chavannes: *la Beauté suprême, la clarté du sujet, l'exquise mesure du geste* ("the supreme beauty, the clarity of subject, the exquisite harmony of gesture"). Here was the sketch of an idyllic nature, which encouraged Cros to fill his scenes with air, and also to acknowledge his generation's naturalistic taste for effects of grottoes, foliage, and watery depths. By means of superimposed planes, Cros succeeded in creating a spacious realm, presided over by the Assembly of Gods.

Two years after starting it in 1903, Cros completed *The Apotheosis of Victor Hugo*, a work that can still be seen in the poet's house in the Place des Vosges (Plate 270). A kind of artistic testament, the Hugo mural relief seems to synthesize all of Cros' formal and thematic concerns: classical Greece; the Pre-Raphaelites and their remote, esoteric charm; Puvis de Chavannes' symbolism and faded harmonies; and Henri Cros' own strong, personal feeling for nature.

Cros' last work, commissioned by the Prince de Wagram, was a monumental chimney for a great château. Choosing to represent *la Belle Saison* ("Summer") symbolically, the artist disclosed his intentions in *L'Art Décoratif:* "The main panel with all its colors evokes the memory or the hope of *la Belle Saison*. The arabesque modeling below, in gray, bluish, or violet grisaille, represents the playful shapes of smoke pouring from the hearth. The terms at either end stand for Wind and Rain overcome, while the blue masks on the architrave signify the atmospheric elements that feed and fan 'the flame' forming both the cornice motif and the chimney's red color." Cros had modeled all the parts, but sudden death prevented his executing the final details. His son Jean was able to complete the work. An example of Jean's own work can be seen in Plate 275.

Thanks to Cros' explanation of *Summer,* we understand how the artist sought, in each of his compositions, to express an idea, a symbol. His friends, far from being strangers to such an approach, were Paul Verlaine, José Maria de Heredia, Stéphane Mallarmé, François Coppée, and Maurice Rollinat—all Parnassians or Symbolists. That is why Cros' oeuvre transcends the classical tradition of ideal beauty to become fully identified with the symbolist movement. His achievement places him among those artist-glassmakers who made an original and lasting contribution to the history of late 19th-century art. An innovator, and even a precursor, who ignored accepted

273. Henri Cros. *Water nymph drawn by a team of sea horses*, c. 1900, height 230 mm/9″, collection Manoukian, Paris. The sea-horse theme, very popular at the time, had an important place in Art Nouveau imagery.

above: 274. Henri Cros. *Amazon*, c. 1895–1900, height 330 mm/13″, collection Manoukian, Paris. The same ideal woman can be found throughout Cros' work, here translated into pâte-de-verre.

right: 275. Jean Cros. *Portrait of Camille Claudel*, c. 1910, height 202 mm/8″, collection F. Marcilhac, Paris. The subject was the great love of Rodin and his inspiration from 1882 to 1900. The sculptor even fashioned the model after which Jean Cros made this rendering into pâte-de-verre.

below left: 276. Albert Dammouse. *Vases in pâte-de-verre*, 1902, height 8 mm/3″ and 100 mm/4″. Musée des Arts Décoratifs, Paris. In the globular vase the delicately shaded tints modulate from the deepest blue to the most tender turquoise. The corolla-cup on the left has curled edges that complete the decoration of large petals.

below right: 277. Albert Dammouse. *Pâte-de-verre cup decorated with flowers in cloisonné enamels*, c. 1904, height 130 mm/5″, collection J.-Cl. Brugnot, Paris.

bottom left: 278. Albert Dammouse. *Bowl and goblet with floral motifs*, c. 1903, Musée des Arts Décoratifs, Paris.

bottom right: 279. Albert Dammouse. *Goblet with lichens*, c. 1903, height 135 mm/5 1/8″, Kunstmuseum, Coll. Hentrich, Düsseldorf.

right: 280. Albert Dammouse. *Nigella of Damascus Calyx-Chalice*, height 380 mm/15″, private collection. This work plays on the contrast between the soft-toned pâte-de-verre dancers and the thorny toughness of the wrought-iron mount, which was designed by Félix Gilon and executed by Frères Nics.

281. Georges Despret. *Head of a Young Girl*, in pâte-de-verre, c. 1903, height 300 mm/11 7/8″, collection A. Lesieutre, Paris. Framed in water-lilies, the face lights up with a tantalizing smile. In the same spirit, Despret made other female masks, including a *Cléo de Mérode*, portraying the famous courtesan of the *fin-de-siècle* era.

ideas to reinvent and revive the ancient technique of pâte-de-verre, Cros not only created an important body of work but also inspired such glass artists as Dammouse, Despret, Décorchemont, Walter, and, a little later, Argy-Rousseau.

Like most great originators, Henri Cros was very discreet about his procedures, saying only that he used colorless powders made from lumps of fired glass. About the all-important problem of how to introduce the various colors so that they do not mix even at low temperatures, he remained absolutely silent.

Cros enjoyed the esteem of his contemporaries, especially that of the Daum brothers. To Antonin Daum, it seemed that Cros avoided technical discussions so as to encourage the public to appreciate his works as artistic rather than technical achievements. In the whole of his production, we feel a strange, indefinable charm, a world where echoes of the past mingle with a unique and poetic sensibility—with "his taste for allegory and symbol," as Madame A. M. Belfort has noted.* The idealized, mysterious Woman, who seems to have pursued Cros through all his compositions, is none other than the personification of a great and dying century (Plates 271, 274).

Normally, a signature appears on Cros' works, but this is not an absolute rule.

282. Henri Cros. *Bust in polychrome pâte-de-verre*, c. 1885, height 180 mm/7″, Musée du Petit Palais, Paris. An excellent portraitist, Cros could render the sweetness and expression of a face even in the difficult pâte-de-verre process.

*"Les pâtes de verre," *Cahiers de la Ceramique et du Feu* (No. 40, 1967, pp. 167–187).

177

right: 283. Albert Dammouse. *Cup with marguerites in pâte d'émail*, c. 1904, height 130 mm/5″, private collection. The decoration stands out in the semitransparent paste.

far right: 284. Albert Dammouse. *Goblet with bluets*, c. 1906, height 130 mm/5″, private collection. The flowers form a garland, cleverly placed around the vessel.

ALBERT DAMMOUSE (1848–1926)

Albert Dammouse was the son of the sculptor and porcelain decorator Pierre-Adolphe Dammouse, and followed in his father's professional footsteps before achieving his own personal success with a remarkably translucent pâte-de-verre. A member of the Sèvres factory staff, the elder Dammouse was in a position to encourage his son while still young to acquire a solid artistic training as a painter and sculptor. The process began at Paris' Ecole Nationale des Arts Décoratifs, but in 1868 young Dammouse entered the Ecole Nationale des Beaux-Arts, there joining the studio of the painter-sculptor François Jouffroy, just as Henri Cros had done. But fascination with materials led Dammouse to become an apprentice and later the collaborator of the ceramist Marc-Louis Solon, called Milès, with whom he remained until 1870, when the older man left for England. Solon, who was known for his experiments in porcelain decoration, taught Dammouse the process of glazed *pâtes d'application* ("applied pastes"), realized in a design traced or modeled by means of a brush loaded with a mixture of oxide coloring materials and water-thinned clay. Having discovered the success of the technique in ceramics, Dammouse conceived the idea of applying it to glass.

In 1869 Dammouse appeared for the first time in official reports, when he obtained the main prize for decorative composition at the Union Centrale des Arts Décoratifs. In 1874, and again in 1878 and 1889 at Paris' Universal Exhibitions, his decorated porcelain pieces received great acclaim. He then began working in close collaboration with the Limoges studios and with the porcelain firm of Charles Haviland in Auteuil. Dammouse provided models and for Haviland created a service in soft paste embellished with birds formed in the round. This was the moment when European modernists were discovering the art of the Far East. Dammouse quite naturally followed the movement, and his ceramics richly reflect the new influence, which would again be felt in the shapes and prototypes that the artist adopted for his production in pâte-de-verre (Plate 276). But right away, beginning in 1882, under the influence of Ernest Chaplet, recently named artistic and technical director of Haviland, Dammouse gave effect to his Orientalism in a material new to him—stoneware.

Finally, in 1892, with the help of brother Edouard, Dammouse opened his own studio at 12 Rue des Fontaines in Sèvres. There he concentrated on stoneware, while also creating in porcelain and faïence. We do not know by what path he came to pâte-de-verre, but conceivably it was the example of Henri Cros that encouraged him to undertake a new kind of experimentation. Whatever the course of development, it permitted Dammouse in 1898 to exhibit small vases shaped as chalices, cups, bowls, and goblets, all made of rather thick, opaque pâte-de-verre and endowed with rippled rims. The decoration, in bold relief, consists of flowers or foliage unfurling from the upper part of the piece. The mat tones remain close to those of Henri Cros, and indeed it would be long before Dammouse could obtain the transparency for which his pâte-de-verre became famous.

The pieces that Dammouse showed at the Universal Exhibition of 1900 created a sudden and dramatic sensation. Having made great technical progress, the artist could now produce a paste both translucent and surprisingly light, but at the cost of excessively thin walls that easily

crumbled and shredded. To remedy this weakness, Dammouse reinforced the rims with a supplementary deposit of vitreous substance. This simply enabled him to make his material ever more delicate, and by 1904 he seems to have been in full command of his technique. Bit by bit, however, the artist succeeded in purifying his material until by 1904 he seems to have gained full command of the pâte-de-verre technology. The decorative effects emerging from the transparent paste and the harmony of tones were most refined, prompting a critic to write that "only his process could give this exquisite coloring." It consisted mainly of blues, often close to turquoise, along with grays and mauves, all delicate hues borrowed from the Impressionist or Symbolist palette, which the glassmaker greatly admired. His modeling causes the decoration to progress subtly from the deepest shades of blue to the palest turquoise (Plate 276 right). Such handling can also be seen in a corolla-cup, a later invention realized with delicately cut and curled edges, below which violet-tinted petals stand out against the contrasting yellow ground (Plate 276 left).

Around 1904 Dammouse tried to produce in pâte-de-verre a decorative effect resembling cloisonné—enamels sectioned by gold wires. His inspiration probably came from the enameled cups by Fernand Thesmar shown at the Exhibition of 1900. Since the metal "cloisons" proved too rigid, and required infinite patience to arrange in a pattern, Dammouse replaced them with a fine and opaque

network of glass paste. After firing the piece in a mold he freed it and filled in the blank "cells" with paste of a different composition, which might be called "enamel paste"* (Plate 277). The unmolded piece was then fired again, this time in the low-temperature muffle kiln. No less than Cros and Décorchement, Dammouse was a solitary worker who failed to leave precise information about his processes. It is thought that, like Thesmar, Dammouse had to fire the object anew for each enamel color, which, of course, would have exacted infinite pains every step of the way, before the piece could be given its final touch. Dammouse also copied Thesmar's forms, which themselves had been derived from Chinese prototypes (Plate 278).

For his decorative designs Albert Dammouse turned to his brother Edouard, who favored light garlands of flowers, foliage, or seaweed stylized in the Art Nouveau manner (Plates 279, 283, 284). Sometimes a fish appears among the swaying seaweed of a Dammouse vase.

Albert Dammouse made two quite exceptional pieces: *Christ on the Cross,* with a wrought-iron mount by Félix Gilon (Plate 285); and *The Nigella of Damascus Calyx-Chalice,* on which Gilon also collaborated, as did the Nics brothers (Plate 280). This spectacular piece is positively astonishing—even troubling—for the contrast it offers between the soft, delicately colored female dancers and the thorny, black-iron enframement set upon an ivory base. This surely must be counted as one of the period's greatest expressions of artistic individuality. It caused a great stir at the 1910 Exposition de Verrerie et de Cristallerie Artistiques.

Dammouse exhibited regularly with considerable and deserved success. Critics praised the supple lines, the

---

* Enamel paste (*pâte d'émail*) is made from the pulverized elements of "glass that is fusible at low temperatures and consists usually of a mixture of different borates and silicates," according to Jules Henrivaux (*La Verrerie au XXe Siècle*). "Under the influence of heat, this basic uncolored mixture combines easily with all, or almost all, of the metallic oxides; according to the nature of the oxides, it takes on different colors that, bright or soft, can be varied at the artist's will."

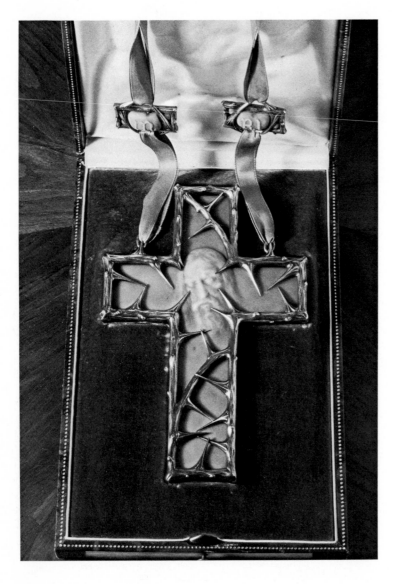

deep, harmonious tones and transparency of his enamel pastes, the simplicity of his décor, and the noble sobriety of his pieces as a whole. The public too appreciated "his remarkable pâtes-de-verre, frail masterpieces made with material possessing the singular beauty of gemstones and with a grace that is peculiarly French."

Dammouse's work remained homogeneous throughout his long career. Eventually, it even began to seem rather out-of-date. Allowing few variations, the artist cultivated a consistent style, all the while that he never ceased perfecting his technique. One critic wrote in 1926: "Fashion never made [Dammouse] forget the idea of a planned decoration. He never failed to create, each year, some important work, such as his much-admired vases in enamel paste, whose appeal long lingers in the memory."

Today the works of Dammouse are still highly prized. Unfortunately, the very fragility of the pieces has left few of them intact, which makes the rare surviving ones all the more precious and expensive.

285. Albert Dammouse. *Christ on the Cross*, c. 1910, height 140 mm/ 5 1/2". Cruciform crown of thorns designed by Félix Gilon and executed by Frères Nics.

RINGEL D'ILLZACH

Ringel d'Illzach's name appears frequently in specialized books on the Art Nouveau era, as one of the artist-researchers in techniques and materials. But little is known about either the man or the artist, and, with very few exceptions, we do not even know what has become of his works.

It is certain, however, that as a tireless investigator d'Illzach tried all kinds of techniques in every possible material so as to express his immediate and deeply felt ideas. In Germany, he was able to study the almost forgotten Renaissance techniques of wax sculpture. As with Henri Cros, working in wax led d'Illzach to seek a more durable material with stable color—pâte-de-verre. Earlier, he had poured bronze, gold, and silver into molds of a refractory material known only to him. These molds enabled the artist to obtain artistic works in the cast itself, without subsequent retouching or correction. Applying the process to pâte-de-verre, d'Illzach found it possible to achieve similar qualities in that material. Contemporary journal accounts tell us that at the Salon of 1899 he exhibited a series of grimacing masks marked by warm color and an unusual delicacy of rendering in translucent pâte-de-verre. These seem to have been spontaneous masterpieces, but the plaque exhibited in 1910 at the Musée Galliéra is the only d'Illzach piece of undoubted authenticity (Plate 286). The signature appears along the right border, written vertically in the Japanese manner. D'Illzach collaborated with Saint-Gobain in the reproduction of medals and, around 1910, with other glassmakers at Meisenthal. It was in this period that he executed three busts entitled *War*, *Victory*, and *Defeat*, all lost and now known only through some glowing reports published at the time.

286. Ringel d'Illzach. *Bust of a Woman*, in polychrome pâte-de-verre, 1899, height 620 mm/24 1/2″, Kunstmuseum, Coll. Hentrich, Düsseldorf. On the right border the signature reads from top to bottom in the manner of Chinese ideograms. Even the smallest details, such as the beauty spot on the subject's shoulder, have been realized in a highly resistant medium.

D'Illzach's molding process, although an artistic technique, caught the interest of industry, which resulted in the large-scale reproduction of a great variety of models. Without losing fineness of detail, the industrialization of d'Illzach's procedures permitted an appreciable reduction in the price of high-quality glass objects.

GEORGES DESPRET (1862–1952)

The name Georges Despret is tied to that of the Glace de Boussois works at Jeumont in northern France, where the artist was the animating spirit in more than one way. A descendant of a long line of the region's master black-smiths, he was in 1884 named director of the Glaceries de Jeumont, a mirror-manufacturing firm, there replacing his uncle, Hector Despret, who had founded the factory in 1859. Thanks to training as an engineer, Georges Despret became an aggressive industrialist and increased the small business rather considerably. In 1908 he took over the Boussois organization and began mass-producing glass, mirrors, plate glass, and wall coverings in pâte-de-verre.

But this industrialist was also a sensitive artist. In 1890 Despret began searching for a new means of expression in an opaque or translucent material that would be both hard and malleable, yet lend itself to subtle gradations of rare and precious tonalities. Already very familiar with glass, he went on to spend nine experimental years in his studio at the factory before he at last hit upon the secret of pâte-de-verre. As we know, Henri Cros had, somewhat earlier, rediscovered this ancient process, but even though Cros and Despret paralleled one another in their research, no exchange of ideas occurred between them. Indeed, their artistic production is very different. Despret created veritable glass sculptures from semitransparent pâte-de-verre, an accomplishment that Cros was able to match only in the exceptional piece. Thus, Despret, for all his business acumen and industrial know-how, developed during the *fin-de-siècle* as one of glassmaking's most creative talents.

At first, however, Despret's material was thick, and his decoration, in very shallow relief, barely detached itself from the mass. The reverse side of a male mask in the Musée de Charleroi, made before 1900, shows the super-imposition of various layers of glass, each with its own color and each the product of a separate firing. Still, it is evident that Despret was attempting to consolidate the object. Then, with pâte-de-verre, which gave him true mastery of the glass medium, he could achieve, straight away and in a single firing, a full and gradated scale of color, value, and contrast.

At the Paris Universal Exhibition of 1900, Despret displayed, along with his mirrors and colored plate glass, some small monochrome, or lightly polychromed, cups in pâte-de-verre, completed during a few days before the opening. Elegant and harmonious, these pieces received much praise before going directly into the collections of the Musée des Arts Décoratifs in Paris and the Industrial Arts Museum in Berlin. In the words of the poet and journalist Armand Sylvestre: "This material seems to contain its own light, to have the pulpy texture of a hyacinth petal, the sweet smoothness of packed snow. It is indeed pâte-de-verre, with its elusive transparency, its real matness, its grain unexceeded by even the finest marbles. . . ."

Taking his cue from Japanese art and the biological world, Despret adopted naturalist themes, which can be seen in vases, or calyx-cups, decorated with beetles, cuttle-fish, and sea horses in the form of handles (Plate 288). A sculpture by Yvonne Serruys provided the model for a fish on a rock, a creature so strange as to seem at the very

287. Georges Despret. *Fish on a Rock*, height 250 mm/9 7/8″, collection F. Marcil-hac, Paris. In pâte-de-verre, after a sculpture by Yvonne Serruys, a fish has been transformed into a fantastic marine monster.

limit of marine monsters (Plate 287). Like Japanese artists, Despret treated his motifs freely, with suppleness and audacity.

For a light and opaque cup in the Hentrich collection Despret liberated a bunch of grapes to stand forth in relief and intertwine in a fantastic way, like a garland. He demonstrated his naturalism also in a whole series of female masks, representing serious, introspective women, or languid, sickly ones, or even young girls with mischievous smiles (Plate 281). According to Gustave Kahn, Despret so pressed his desire for realism that on one occasion he even gave a living toad a coat of pâte-de-verre. With the heartless objectivity of the true laboratory scientist, he fired this real-life mold and thus obtained the greatest possible naturalism!

Interested in the effects of materials, Despret often wanted to prove that he could reproduce the grain of Parian marble, or even of bronze, the latter most notably in a statuette "that would be bronze were it not pâte-de-verre imitating the colors and reflections of bronze." He also hoped to use pâte-de-verre to imitate gems, such as onyx, obsidian, or agate, and to endow them with the nacreous quality of a woman's skin. A small cup belonging to the Musée des Arts Décoratifs simply vibrates by virtue of contrasting colors and lapis-lazuli marblings (Plate 289). Three pieces belonging to the Conservatoire des Arts et Métiers also testify to Despret's extraordinary skill, for in them the master juxtaposed the roughness of Oriental ceramics with fine carving in what appears to be cornelian (Plate 290). In these mold-blown pieces he created the effect of stoneware by means of crushed colored glass lay-

ered into the mass or attached to its surface. Despret even managed to emulate the blotches and imperfections normally found in Japanese ceramics. For another vase he blew an iridescent material, which metallized once subjected to the reducing action of fire. Meanwhile, Despret tended toward more severe and classical shapes, away from the freer, fanciful forms characteristic of Art Nouveau. Even while taking his inspiration from the Far East, the artist clung to the austere, hieratic ideals of Greece and Egypt. Thus, from the Despret atelier came statuettes imitating the figures of Tanagra, also Hellenistic torsos and seated scribes.

A good administrator, Despret employed competent collaborators, among whom must be counted Géo Nicollet, an early artistic advisor, as well as Yvonne Serruys, Pierre Le Faguays. Charles Toché, and M. de Glori. Like Cros and Décorchemont, Despret worked only in a craftsmanly way, which means that no two pieces by him are identical.

The Despret studios and factory were destroyed during World War I, which brought bombardment to the Musée Communal de Jeumont, resulting in the loss of the collection Despret had made of the best specimens from his artistic production. After the 1914-18 interruption, the business continued until the 1930s, when it ceased altogether in 1937.

Through his original and highly dynamic personality, Despret gave the art of pâte-de-verre a new stimulus and development. He signed with his full name, in gold or blue, and sometimes supplemented the signature with a number or a monogram.

below: 291. François Décorchemont. (a) *Vase decorated with seaweed and shellfish in pâte-de-verre*, c. 1912, height 160 mm/6 1/8″; (b) *Vase with pine cones in semitransparent pâte-de-verre*, c. 1912, height 160 mm/6 1/8″. Collection A. Lesieutre, Paris. Beginning in 1908, the pieces become thicker, thanks to the lost-wax process, an exceedingly difficult technique taken up by only a few glassmakers. It left the material looking crackled, and in (b) with veins or trails of blue.

right: 292. François Décorchemont. *Vase decorated with masks, pine cones, and foliage*, 1910 or 1911, height 170 mm/6 5/8″, collection F. Marcilhac, Paris. So rich is the relief in this mold-formed piece that the pâte-de-verre looks carved.

left: **293.** François Décorchemont. *Cup with ferns,* 1906, height 87 mm/ 3 3/8″, Musée des Arts Décoratifs, Paris. At this date Décorchemont's *pâte d'email* was very light and fragile. For the surface relief, the artist used Dammouse's "stamping" technique.

below: **294.** François Décorchemont. *Cup with ferns,* 1913, height 115 mm/4 1/5″, collection F. Marcilhac, Paris. The theme is that seen in Plate 273, but now, by means of the lost-wax process, amplified in thicker material and with fresher colors.

François Décorchemont (1880–1971)

Francois Décorchemont was born in the Norman town of Conches on May 26, 1880. Painter, ceramist, and sculptor, he owes his fame above all to the work he accomplished as a master glassmaker. Décorchemont enjoyed a propitious start, coming as he did from a family of artists. His father was a sculptor who worked under the academician Jean-Léon Gérôme, creating works mainly on commission or for exhibition at the annual Paris Salons. He later became a professor of sculpture at the Académie des Arts Décoratifs. As for François' mother, née Laumônier, she could count painters, sculptors, and decorators among her ancestors all the way back to the 17th century.

Until the age of twelve, François lived in his maternal grandparents' house in Conches, where the constant talk about art had a deep and lasting influence on his life. Then in 1892, the boy joined his parents in Paris, at 12 Rue Ganneron near Place Clichy, which placed him at the very center of Parisian artistic life. The studies he had begun in Conches now continued at the College Chaptal, and, after 1896, at the Ecole des Arts Décoratifs. There young Décorchemont received his diploma in 1900. Enthusiastic about such Impressionist masters as Manet and Pissarro, he made painting his vocation, exhibiting canvases at the 1903 Salon des Artistes Français. After such a preparation, it should not surprise that Décorchemont conceived of his glass and ceramic works as paintings and sculptures.

With increasing curiosity about all means of plastic expression, Décorchemont experimented with leather bookbinding, and even here he managed to give free reign to his strong pictorial sense. Simultaneously, he also took up the "arts of fire" and tried his hand with stoneware, baking the pieces, to the great distress of his neighbors, in his room heater on Rue Ganneron! Needless to say, the results failed to satisfy him, and in 1902 he launched upon serious research into technical and artistic issues that soon plunged him into a life-long obsession with pâte-de-verre.

Décorchemont made his first pâte-de-verre pieces in 1903, using the long-lost ceramic-cum-glass technique rediscovered in the 19th century by Henri Cros. Here, at last, was the medium through which he could develop his interest in shapes and colors and express his richly inventive temperament. "Pâte-de-verre? Crushed glass, refired for a long time and thus reshaped. There are molds, one mixes the colors, fills the molds, then bakes them at 1250æ for twelve hours. One makes one's own material—that's all." Who else could have defined the process with such modesty and simplicity?

Up to 1910 Décorchemont fired in a coke furnace at his father's studio. Eventually, he settled for good in Conches and there had a petrol-fired furnace installed to his own specifications. Although archaic in appearance, the kiln allowed him to regulate the flame at will and thus assure a regular firing. From that time forward, he never left Conches, which made him seem a medieval personality misplaced in the modern world. But while solitary, Décorchemont was not a recluse, for he remained in friendly contact with the artistic world of his time, without, however, sacrificing his own, quite individual approach. Somewhat in the spirit of John Ruskin and Japanese artists, Décorchemont preached a return to nature, a doctrine he practiced by collecting rare insects and making casts of ornamental plants. In an oeuvre that is coherent and very personal, and whose inspiration he constantly renewed, Décorchemont regularly mixed echoes of shapes from Ro-

295. François Décorchemont. *Esterelle*, before 1905, height 250 mm/ 9 7/8″, Musée d'Art Moderne, Paris. Very few of the artist's statuettes in pâte-de-verre have survived, especially from his first period. The costume seems to have been inspired by the Italian Renaissance.

man Imperial silver and from Egyptian and Oriental glass with his own keen sense of modernity.

Décorchemont created important works right up to his death on February 19, 1971, in, of course, Conches. His production went from decorative abundance to the most reductive simplicity.

Décorchemont's Works and Techniques

The work turned out by Décorchemont before 1914 represents only a small fraction of his total production. It is of interest, however, in two different ways: as a reflection of the period, and as the prelude to the great compositions that would later come from this master.

In his first pieces, made between 1903 and 1908, Décorchemont quite naturally expressed the eagerness of a sculptor to discover a vitrifiable material capable of giving effect to his curiously pictorial tendencies (Plate 295). These works are thin and opaque; thus, they raise questions concerning the degree to which they may be pâte-de-verre or soft-paste ceramic (Plate 293). Adopting the simple, traditional shapes of cups and goblets, Décorchemont made them personal by means of stylized decorations of flowers and animals mixed with masks, putti, shellfish, and colored marblings (Plate 296). The silhouettes can be clear and perfect, or yet lost in the very thickness of the paste. Painterly and nuanced, the colors reflect the artist's unique sensibility, which favored mauves, roses, blues, and pale, soft sea-greens.

A complete artist, Décorchemont was not content simply to design shapes; he even made the colored glass from which he mixed his paste. To do this, he added metallic oxides to clear, pulverized glass* or crystal. Once he had such a compound, he fired it in crucibles that he had also fashioned with his own hands, drying them in the sun and "reviving" (lightly firing) them in the furnace. The blocks of colored glass formed in the crucibles were now themselves crushed.

To shape his piece, Décorchemont employed a technique called "stamping." A new fireclay mold was made in the desired way, with the decoration worked in intaglio. Over this interior surface went the "slip" of powdered glass bound with a liquid, which Décorchemont had made from quince pips according to a "recipe" borrowed from a 16th-century monk—Brother Théophile—known as an alchemist. Upon firing, the pips acted like a glue, but disappeared without a trace, having in no way altered the colors.

When the paste had dried, Décorchemont took the formed piece from the mold and worked it *à cru* ("raw"; that is, before firing), using not only a term but also a technique normal in faïence. He then went to the mouffle furnace (set at a low temperature of about 500°) and fired the piece in a mold of lime made from marble found in the elder Décorchemont's sculpture studio. Retrieving the fired object from the kiln, the artist colored it with a brush dipped in metallic oxides, after which he subjected it to a final firing of about twenty-two hours at 1200°. To prevent breakage, the cooling had to be done slowly, in fact spread over four or five days.

A laborious and risk-ridden technique, the procedures followed by Décorchemont in his pâte-de-verre allowed only a few successes, no more possibly than two or three out of twenty tries. This makes the completed works all the more precious.

By 1908, following three years of experimentation, Décorchemont had mastered a new technique that made possible pieces that are both thicker and semitransparent (Plate 291). This was a lost-wax process, resembling that used by sculptors to cast bronze. The artist commenced by making a maquette in plaster, carefully scupted in complete detail. He then covered the form with wax to the thickness required for the final object. On top of the wax, he next applied plaster to make an outer mold. After covering the whole in fireclay, he heated the assemblage to melt the wax, which ran out through conduits made in the outer shells. Into the space now left between the mold and the counter-mold went the glass paste colored with metallic oxides. Fired at 1150–1250°, the molded piece had to cool slowly and progressively over a period of eight days. The molds could then be demolished, revealing the pâte-de-verre piece. It was then polished and finished to a smooth state, especially after 1920.

The shapes that Décorchemont could achieve with this technique are varied, but as they increased in power and size, they also gained in suppleness (Plates 292, 294, 297). Up to 1914, the artist almost invariably chose decorative themes from the biological world. The colors, as we have seen, were prepared by the artist himself, who followed tradition and used cobalt for blue, copper sulphate or gold salts thinned in aqua regia (Cassius purple) for the reds, and finally uranium and platinum for yellow and gray.

*He prepared the glass himself, all the way from its most basic components—silica and a melting agent.

But the genius of the master glassmaker revealed itself in the way the colors were handled, in the proportions and in the special or original mixtures, as well as in the manner of placing the colors so that they would not mingle during the firing.

In the beginning, Décorchemont used clear glass of his own making, but in 1912 he began buying crystal from Saint-Denis. Later he obtained it from Daum.

Décorchemont was one of the few glassmakers to have employed the lost-wax process, which yielded either unique pieces or precious few examples from the same model. Even so, the artist loved to make a joke: *Je ne suis ni verrier, ni vitraillier, et pourtant j'ai fait du verre et du vitrail* ("I am neither a glassmaker nor a stained-glass-window-maker, and yet I have made both glass and stained-glass windows").

Signatures and Marks on the Glass of François Décorchemont

Usually the pieces are signed with the artist's full name by means of a stamp formed like a shell, which is the device of the town of Conches, a name derived from the Latin for *coquille* or "shell": *concha.* In addition to the signature stamp, there could also be marks, letters, or numbers that permit dating or, more likely, to place the individual work in a given period.

For these details, and those that follow, we are indebted to Mme François Décorchemont, who for many years worked as her husband's collaborator:

- From 1903 to 1909 inclusive, the pieces are marked with a letter followed by a number. It should be noted that the letters are not in alphabetical order. Few works survive from this period. On the earliest (1903–04), a date

in India ink sometimes appears, in addition to the stamp.
- From 1910 to 1911 inclusive, the rather rare pieces are marked with two letters followed by a number.
- From December 1912 to November 1921, the pieces are marked with the stamp, but beyond that only with numbers, from 1 to 999.
- From November 1921 to December 1924, they are marked with a zero followed by a number, from 01 to 0999.
- From November 1924 to August 1927, we find the letter A followed by a number, from A 1 to A 999.
- From August 1927 to November 1930, the letter B is followed by a number, from B 1 to B 999.
- From November 1930 to May 1939, the letter C is followed by a number, from C 1 to C 433.
- From July 1945 to January 1971, the letter D is followed by a number, from D 1 to D 507.

Some pieces dating from 1945 also bear the Cross of Lorraine. Certain other pieces marked "M. A." were the personal property of Mme M. A. Décorchemont. On the stained-glass windows, only the stamp appears, without letters or numbers.

above: 296. François Décorchemont. *Small cup in pâte d'email*, 1903, height 60 mm/2 1/2", Musée d'Art Moderne, Paris. The artist took the shape from a Roman silver cup recovered at Boscoreale.

right: 297. François Décorchemont. *Vase with Silenus masks*, 1914, height 195 mm/7 5/8", collection F. Marcilhac, Paris. The bubbles and other irregularities characteristic of pâte-de-verre were deliberately cultivated by the artist as an expressive device. Décorchemont treated the mask theme early in his career, but just after World War I he returned to it with great frequency.

CONCLUSION

Throughout this discussion we have endeavored to create understanding and appreciation of the achievement of France's late-19th-century glassmakers, whose production includes many true works of art. In their own time, these masters enjoyed esteem only among an enthusiastic elite of poets and connoisseurs, who admired both the talent and the technical virtuosity of the *verriers*. The general public remained largely unaware of the remarkable developments in glass. Yet, Emile Gallé and his associates participated fully in the most important artistic currents flowing through that climactic moment in French art—the *fin de siècle*.

Time has finally assuaged the passions that fueled the great artistic revolutions of the late 19th century, with the consequence that the innovative works in glass can now take their rightful place, not only in the history of the decorative arts, but also in the art of all time. In their great generative force, in their boldness and individuality, the glassmakers produced aesthetic objects that can hold their own with the best of the bronzes, marbles, and gems created by the Renaissance and even antiquity. Indeed, French art glass of the period 1860-1914 is at home wherever human genius has given expression to its capacity for reverie and poetry, mystery and beauty.

GLOSSARY

Within the definitions *italics* have been used to indicate terms that themselves are defined in the glossary.

agate glass An opaque glass imitating such semiprecious stones as agate, chalcedony, onyx, jasper, and malachite.

annealing The process whereby glass, after firing, is taken to a certain temperature and then slowly but uniformly cooled in the *lehr*. By eliminating stress caused by uneven cooling, annealing toughens glass and makes it more resistant to breakage.

aventurine glass A yellowish, translucent glass flecked throughout with sparkling copper particles. An imitation of aventurine quartz, it was developed in Venice in the 17th or 18th century.

blowpipe The hollow iron rod about 1.60m (5'3") long that is the glassblower's principal tool. After *gathering* the molten glass upon the tube's thickened end, the craftsman blows through a mouthpiece, which has a wooden sleeve, to form the material into a bubble.

bullion bars Horizontal steel bars upon which the glassmaker leans his *blowpipe* or *pontil*, held in his left hand, while shaping the glass with his right hand.

cameo glass Glass layered or *cased* in two or more colors to create a design consisting of a form in one color relieved by carving and therefore set off against a ground of a different color.

cased glass Glass made of two or more fused layers of glass, with each layer an independent color. Once the shaped and shell-like outer layer (overlay) has been placed in a mold, a second *paraison* is blown into it, whereupon the composite piece must be removed from the mold and reheated until the two layers have fused. For additional casing, the process can be repeated. Cased glass has a thick overlay, in contrast to the thin overlay of *flashed* glass.

chair The bench on which the glassmaker sits while working the glass. It is equipped with slightly sloping arms, called *bullion bars*, that permit the craftsman to rest his *blowpipe* as he constantly rotates it back and forth in the process of forming the molten glass.

Chinese red According to their own explanations, Monot and Stumpf obtained Chinese red with a mixture of copper and gold fused between two layers of glass.

crackled glass Glass shot through with webs of small cracks and fissures, all refracting light and creating the effect of great sparkle. The simplest method of obtaining crackled glass is to plunge the molten object into cold water.

crucible The *pot*, or fireproof clay mold, in which the ingredients of glass are fused.

crystal Clear glass made from varying proportions of pure sand, potash, and lead oxide or pure lead. Today crystal, for it to be called such, must contain at least 24 percent lead oxide.

cullet Broken glass and remnants left on the *blowpipe* that are added to fresh ingredients and melted to make a new batch of glass.

diamond-point engraving The process of decorating glass by scoring it with a diamond point.

églomisé A decorative technique associated with Jean-Baptiste Glomy, an 18th-century French draftsman and framer whose shop was famous in Paris. As the enframement of prints or gouaches, he applied golden threads to the underside of the protective glass and bound them with a ground of black varnish. In reality, however, this technique is much older, having been known even to the Romans. After engraving with diamond point on gold leaf, the decoration was then fused between two layers of glass. In the 18th century, Bohemia produced a large amount of *verre églomisé*.

émaux-bijoux Invented by Gallé, these were translucent enamels built up in successive layers and fused to a foil of precious metal, which was then applied by heat to the glass piece.

enamel glass Glass decorated with vitreous fusible substances pigmented by metallic oxides or other coloring agents. Once applied with a brush, the enamel pigments are fused to the glass surface by low temperature.

engraving The technique of decorating glass by cutting or scoring the surface with a diamond point, a metal needle, or a rotating wheel. Related to *etching*.

etching As in engraving, to etch glass is to decorate it by cutting into the surface of the material, but in etching this is accomplished by means of acid rather than with a sharp-pointed implement.

filigree Decoration in which one or more opaque white or colored glass rods or threads are sunk into the vitreous mass during the time this material is being fired. The threads or rods can also be applied as relief.

flash To fuse a thin overlay of glass onto a thicker shell or main body of a glass object. The process involves dipping the basic form in molten glass and then reheating the glass-coated form. If the flash, or thin overlay, is of a different color, it can be carved to produce the patterned effect of *cameo glass*. A process of *layering*. See also *cased glass*.

flux Basic oxide—borax, potash, or soda, among others—added to the vitreous ingredients in order to facilitate melting by lowering the fusion point for silica.

frosting A mat, translucent surface obtained by attacking glass with acid, a rotating wheel, or a strong jet of sand.

furnace The heated chamber in which pots or crucibles are placed for fusing the vitreous ingredients.

gather See *gathering*.

gathering That phase of the glassmaking process in which the craftsman drips the end of his *blowpipe* into the *pot* or *crucible* to collect a blob of molten glass (a gather) sufficient in size to form the desired object.

gathering iron A solid iron rod used to dip into the *pot* or *crucible* for the purpose of gathering molten glass that is not to be blown.

glass A noncrystalline substance, usually transparent but sometimes translucent, created by fusing at a temperature of about 1400°C., silica (sand), an alkali (potash or soda), and lime or lead oxide. When molten, glass is plastic and can be shaped by blowing and molding; when cooled from a molten state, it is ductile and can be shaped by rolling, drawing out, and bending; and when cold, it is glyptic and can be modified or decorated by cutting, *engraving*, or *etching*.

hammering A technique developed at Daum whereby a glass surface is wheel-engraved in facets to create an effect like that of hammered metal.

196

Extrait du rapport fait par M. de Luynes au nom du comité des arts économiques, sur les verreries et cristaux décorés par de nouveaux procédés de M. Monot, de Pantin (Seine). (Bulletin de la Sté d'encouragement pour l'industrie nationale) (France).

« Monsieur Monot s'est aussi préoccupé de cristallerie de luxe, indépendamment de la fabrication courante obtenue dans les meilleures conditions de qualité et de forme, il a créé des genres nouveaux qui ont vivement frappé l'attention à leur apparition. Nous citerons surtout ses pièces craquelées à reflets métalliques et ses feuilles métalliques vermeil. —

« Voici en quoi consiste la fabrication des vases craquelés à reflets métalliques :

« Une masse de cristal ayant reçu sa première forme, est recouverte extérieurement d'une couche de verre à l'argent et d'une couche de cristal mince, ce qui constitue un verre triple dont la surface est ensuite dorée au four. Après quoi, au moyen du soufflage, on applique à l'extérieur une couche mince de verre à l'argent. —

« La pièce, chauffée au rouge, étant plongée dans l'eau froide, la couche vitreuse dorée se trouve recouverte de craquelures qui mettent à jour entre elles la surface du verre à l'argent placée au dessous.

« C'est alors qu'au moyen d'un chalumeau spécial on dirige un jet de gaz décarburé qui, projeté sur le verre à l'argent, le réduit en produisant une belle irisation métallique à l'intérieur

« du vase et entre les craquelures. Nous devons
« ajouter que le verre à l'argent, employé dans cette
« fabrication, est encore une création de Mʳ Monot.

« Avant lui, le verre à l'argent ne s'obtenait que
« par cémentation; c'est lui qui, le premier, a préparé
« le verre à l'argent coloré dans la masse, dont il s'est
« servi en 1867 dans sa petite usine de l'Exposition.

« Les feuilles vermeil s'obtiennent par un
« procédé qui est, en quelque sorte, la réciproque du
« précédent. Une paraison recouverte à l'intérieur
« d'une couche mince de verre cuivreux et présentant
« en ses divers points, des épaisseurs différentes, est
« reproduite chaude dans un moule en deux parties,
« ayant un écartement convenable. Un chalumeau
« au gaz, placé au bout de la canne, sert à y intro-
« duire le gaz, sous une pression suffisante pour
« obtenir le moulage; mais le gaz réduit en même
« temps le verre à base de cuivre et produit à sa
« surface une métallisation très remarquable.

« C'est, en réalité un procédé de réduction analogue
« au précédent, avec cette différence que le gaz agit
« à l'intérieur de la pièce au lieu d'être appliqué
« à l'extérieur.

« Nous avons encore à citer le genre cristal de
« roche avec dessins en reliefs, et une fabrication
« d'aventurine très réussie.

« Tous ces nouveaux genres ont paru à l'Exposition
« de 1878, où ils ont obtenu le plus grand et le plus
« légitime succès. L'exposition générale de Mʳ Monot
« est, en effet, une de celles qui ont été le plus remarquées.

(Signé) Mʳ de Luynes.
(Rapporteur.)

left and right: Report of M. de Luynes to the Comité des Arts économiques on the various technical innovations of Monot. This former employee of the Cristallerie de Lyons would found his own company, the Cristalleries de Pantin. His production distinguished itself more for craftsmanship and technical novelty than for creative originality.

incrustation A decorative effect achieved when precious materials, pieces of glyptic glass, impurities, etc., have been imbedded in molten glass. See *occlusion*.

intarsia See *marqueterie de verre*.

intercalary decoration A sophisticated technique and a specialty of Daum, wherein a multilayered piece richly decorated by enameling, carving, or etching is encased in a new layer of glass and then carved to reveal the decoration below. The process resembles Gallé's *marqueterie de verre*.

latticinio Derived from the Italian *latte* ("milk"), this term designates clear glass made to look filigreed either by the addition of tin oxide or arsenic to the molten material, or by imbedding therein threads or rods of glass. Latticinio was developed in 16th-century Venice.

layering A general term for the processes of fusing two or more layers of glass. See *cased glass* and *flash*.

lehr A reheating oven or furnace used for *annealing* glass, the lehr is tunnel-shaped, long (12–15m or 39–49'), brick-lined, and fired at one end. As the glass objects move through the lehr, conveyed on iron wagons pulled by chains, they are gradually reheated and then uniformly cooled.

mallet A wooden glassmaker's tool in the form of a mallet, used to shape hot glass.

marqueterie de verre Taking his inspiration from wood marquetry, or *intarsia*, Gallé invented "glass marquetry," a process for obtaining local colors that are integral with the continuous mass of a glass object. After applying thin laminations of hot colored glass to a *paraison*, and arranging them like mosaic in accordance with a prepared design, Gallé fired the piece, often added a final layer of clear crystal, and then carved or etched the surface to reveal the design deep within the various layers.

marver A smooth slab of marble or cast iron on which the glassmaker can roll and shape his *paraison*.

metal A glassmaker's term for *glass*.

milk glass Glass rendered white and opaque by the addition of tin oxide and thereby given the appearance of Chinese white porcelain.

millefiori Italian for "thousand flowers," the term designates glass ornamented by the process of imbedding in clear, molten medium a variety of small multicolored glass rods or threads, often arranged in symmetrial, flowerlike designs.

mold blowing Forming glass by blowing a gather into a refractory, or fireclay, mold.

occlusion An air bubble or foreign particle, such as gold dust, trapped for decorative purposes within the mass of a glass object.

opaline Glass opacified to a translucent or opalescent state by the addition of tin oxide and ashes of calcined bone (clattimo). Not to be confused with *milk glass*.

paraison On the end of the *blowpipe*, the *gather*, mass, or blob of molten glass after it has been blown into its first form or bubble. Other terms are "skull cap" and "chemise."

pâte-de-verre French for "glass paste," the term describes a material produced by mixing (while cold) crushed glass, powdered enamels, and a binder, usually water. The paste thus formed is applied to the inner relief surface of a mold, after which the mold and its vitreous contents are fired, causing the elements of the pâte-de-verre to fuse and cohere. Once the mold is removed, the glass form stands free like a sculpture, fully colored in the mass.

patination A process developed by Gallé to take aesthetic advantage of the devitrified or pocked surface caused by an impurity like dust in the course of firing. By systematically inducing surface devitrification, Gallé created the crepelike effect that he called "patination."

pincers A glassmaker's tool used for opening the *paraison* and for threading or squeezing molten glass into decorative patterns.

polishing Endowing glass with brilliance and finish by means of wood, cork, or felt wheels.

pontil The iron rod on which the still-molten glass piece is given its final form, after it has been tentatively shaped on the *blowpipe*.

pot The *crucible*.

preliminary heating A technique for removing moisture from vitreous substances before placing them in the *crucible*. It involves heating in the *lehr*.

preparing Rolling the *gather* of glass on the *marver* preparatory to blowing it.

shears A glassmaker's tool used to cut or trim molten glass.

silica A mineral that constitutes one of the essential ingredients of glass. For glassmaking purposes, the most common form of silica is sand. Also available in rocks, pebbles, and flint.

soda The alkali ingredient of glass, soda (or soda carbonate) functions as a flux to reduce the fusion point of *silica*.

strass A brilliant, highly refractive, lead-rich glass suitable for making artificial gemstones. The process was developed by Georges-Frédéric Strass (1701–73), an Alsatian jeweler established in Paris.

Wiederkomm German for "come again," the term designates a type of large glass, enamel-decorated beaker (a Humpen) made in Germany during the 16th and 17th centuries and used for drinking beer or wine on saying "goodbye" or "au revoir."

working hole An opening made in the furnace for *gathering* glass.

BIBLIOGRAPHY

Amic, Yolande, *L'Opaline française.* s.l. 1955.
Annales des Musées de France, 1970. Paris 1970.
Appert, Léon, and Henrivaux, Jules, *La Verrerie depuis vingt ans.* Paris 1894.
Art et curiosité. Publication of the Syndicat national des antiquaires négociants en objets d'art... Paris.
Art décoratif, 1898–1899, 1900, 1902, 1904, 1905, 1907–1908.
Art et Décoration, 1897, 1899, 1909, 1926. Paris.
Art de France. Annual review of l'Art ancien et moderne. Paris.
Art et Industrie. Periodical on the fine and decorative arts, 1908–1910, 1912–1914. Paris.
Arts de France (review). Paris.
Arts et manufactures. Monthly review of the association of former students of the Ecole Centrale des Arts et Manufactures. Paris.
Arwas, Victor, *Glass: Art Nouveau to Art Deco.* New York 1977.
Barrelet, James, *La Verrerie en France, de l'époque gallo-romaine jusqu'à nos jours.* Paris 1953.
Bastenaire-Daudenart, F., L'Art de la vitrification, ou Traité élémentaire, théorique et pratique de la fabrication du verre. Paris 1825.
Bayard, Emile, *L'Art appliqué français d'aujourd'hui: meubles, ferronnerie, céramique, verrerie, tissus, etc.* Paris 1925.
Bayard, Emile, *Le Style moderne.* Paris 1919.
Belfort, Anne-Marie, "Les pâtes de verre d'Henri Cros," *Cahiers de la Céramique et des Arts du Feu,* No. 39. Sèvres 1967.
Bontemps, Georges, *Peinture sur verre au XIXe siècle.* Paris 1845.
Bontemps, Georges, *Guide du verrier, traité historique et pratique de la fabrication des verres, cristaux, vitraux.* Paris 1868.
Bulletin de l'Union Centrale des Arts Décoratifs, 1874–1879, 1903. Paris.
Cassou, Jean, *Les Sources du XXe siècle.* Paris 1961.
Catalogue de l'Exposition d'Art décoratif et industriel lorrain. s.l. 1894.
Catalogue de l'Exposition de Verrerie et de Cristallerie du Musée Galliéra. s.l. 1910.
Catalogue de Lemoine et fils horticulteurs 1899–1900. s.l.n.d.
Catalogue de la vente de la collection Roger Marx. s.l. 1914.
Catalogue de la vente de la bibliothèque de M. de Montesquiou du 23–25 avril 1923 à l'Hôtel Drouot. Paris 1923.
Catalogue de la vente de la bibliothèque de M. de Montesquiou du 2–4 avril 1924. Paris 1924.
Chambon, Raymond, *Depuis 3000 ans... le verre.* Charleroi 1970.
Charpentier, Françoise-Thérèse, "L'Ecole de Nancy et la Renaissance de l'art décoratif en France," *Médecine de France,* July 1964. — "L'Art de Gallé a-t-il été influencé par Baudelaire?" *Gazette des Beaux-Arts,* June 1963.
Chavance, René, *L'Art français depuis vingt ans—La Céramique et la verrerie.* Paris 1928.
Coffignal, Louis, *Verres et émaux.* Paris 1900.
Comte, Jules, *L'Art à l'Exposition universelle de 1900.* Paris 1900.
Demoriane, Hélène, "Le Cas étrange de Monsieur Gallé," *Connaisance des Arts,* August 1960.
Diderot, Denis, *Encyclopédie,* Vol. XVII. Paris 1782.
Didron, Edouard, and Clémandot, Louis, *Exposition universelle et internationale de 1878 à Paris—Rapport sur les cristaux, la verrerie et les vitraux.* Paris 1880.
Didron, Edouard, *Rapport d'ensemble sur les arts décoratifs à l'Exposition universelle de 1878.* Paris 1882.
Dufrène and Demont, *Rapport sur l'Exposition universelle de 1878.— L'Art industriel.* Paris 1882.
Duret-Robert, François, "Ecole de Nancy, Gallé," *Connaissance des Arts,* Sept. 1970, June and August 1971, Jan. 1972. —"Ecole de Nancy, Daum," *Connaissance des Arts,* April 1971, Oct. and Nov. 1971, Nov. 1972, Nov. 1973. — "Ecole de Nancy, Décorchemont." *Connaissance des Arts,* June and July 1973. — "Ecole de Nancy, Victor Prouvé," *Connais-*

sance des Arts, April 1974.
Esnault, Louis, "L'Exposition de Bruxelles," *L'Illustration,* 7 August 1897. Paris
Exposition lorraine de l'Ecole de Nancy au Pavillon de Marsan 1903. s.l.n.d.
Fourcaud, Louis de, *Emile Gallé.* Paris 1903.
Gallé, Emile, *Ecrits pour l'Art.* Paris 1908.
Garner, Philippe, *Émile Gallé.* New York 1976.
Garnier, Edouard, *Histoire de la verrerie et de l'émaillerie,* Tours 1886.
Garnier, Edouard, *Le Verre à l'Exposition de 1900.* s.l. 1900.
Gerspach, Edouard, *L'Art de la verrerie,* Paris 1885.
Gillet, Louis, "Les poèmes du verre," *Revue hebdomadaire,* Oct. 1910.
Le Goût moderne, No. 1. Paris 1926.
Grand, P.M., "Poésie du cristal," *Jardin des Arts,* Nos. 97–98, Paris 1963.
Grover, Ray and Lee, *Carved and Decorated European Art Glass.* Rutland (Vermont) 1970.
Grover, Ray and Lee, *European Art Glass Nouveau.* Rutland (Vermont) 1967.
Guerrand, Roger H., *L'Art Nouveau en Europe,* prefaced by *Le Modern style d'ou je suis,* by Aragon. Paris 1965.
Havard, Henry, *Les Arts de l'ameublement—La Verrerie.* Paris 1894.
Havard, Henry, *Histoire et philosophie des styles (architecture, ameublement, décoration).* Paris 1899–1900.
Heiligenstein, Auguste-Claude, *Précis de décoration dans les arts du feu. Verrerie, Porcelaine. Faïence.* Paris 1957.
Henrivaux, Jules, *La Verrerie au XXe siècle.* Paris 1911.
Henrivaux, Jules, *Le Verre et le cristal.* Paris 1897.
Henrivaux, Jules, *Verre et Verrerie.* Paris 1894.
Henrivaux, Jules, *L'Art et Industrie à l'Exposition du Musée Galliéra 1910.* Paris 1910.
Hilschenz, Helga, *Das Glas des Jugendstils,* Düsseldorf 1973.
Houtart, Eugène, *Rapport sur l'Exposition de 1900.* Paris 1901.
Houtart, Charles, "L'industrie de la verrerie dans le Nord de la France du XIXe siècle à ce jour," *Le Verre,* Nos. 10–12 (1924), 2 (1925).
Hubert, Eugène François d', *Les verres et cristaux, le diamant et les gemmes.* Paris 1904.
Illustration économique et financière, 1925.
Internationales Jugendstilgas. Munich 1969.
Janneau, Gaston, *Modern glass,* London 1931.
Jean, René, *Les Arts de la terre: céramique, verrerie, émaillerie, mosaïque, vitrail.* Paris 1911.
Julia de Fontenelle, Jean-Sébastien and Malepeyre, F. (revised by H. Bertran), *Nouveau Manuel complet du verrier et du fabricant de glaces, cristaux...* Encyclopédie Roret. Paris 1900.
Legrans, *La Verrerie française à l'Exposition de 1900.* s.l. 1900.
Lemonnier, *Extraits du Bulletin des Amis de l'Université de Nancy.* Paris 1901.
La Libre Esthétique—Catalogue de la deuxième Exposition de Bruxelles. Bruxelles 1895.
La Lorraine, 1901–1904.
Mackearin, George S. and Helen, *Two Hundred Years of American Blown Glass.* New York 1950.
Mariacher, Giovanni, *Art italien: le verre,* trans. by M.P. and Ch. Bonlay. Paris 1961.
Martin, René, *Exposition internationale de Milan, 1906. Section française. Arts décoratifs.* Paris 1910.
Martin, René, *Exposition universelle et internationale de Gand (1913)— Verres et cristaux.* Paris s.d.
Marx, Roger, *L'Art à Nancy en 1882...* Nancy 1883.
Marx, Roger, *La Décoration et l'art industriel à l'Exposition Universelle de 1889.* Paris 1890.
Marx, Roger, *La Décoration et les industries d'art à l'Exposition*

Universelle de 1900. Paris 1901.

Marx, Roger, "Gallé," *Art et Décoration*, August 1911. Paris.

Meixmoron de Dombasle, Charles de, *Académie de Stanislas. Réponse du président au récipiendaire, M. Emile Gallé.* Nancy 1900.

Michel, Andreé, *Histoire de l'art depuis les premiers temps chrétiens jusqu'à nos jours.* Paris 1905-1929.

Molinier, Emile, *Histoire des arts appliqués à l'industrie, du Ve à la fin du XVIIIe siècle.* Vol. III. Paris 1891.

Molinier, Emile, *Exposition rétrospective des Beaux-Arts et des Arts décoratifs en 1900.* Paris 1907.

Mourey, Georges, *Histoire générale de l'art français de la Révolution à nos jours.* Paris 1922.

Newman, Harold, *An Illustrated Dictionary of Glass.* London 1977.

Painter, George D., *Marcel Proust*, trans. by G. Gattani and R.P. Vial. Paris. 1966.

Pazaurek, Gustav E., *Moderne Gläser. Leipzig 1901.*

Pazaurek, Gustav E., *Kunstgläser der Gegenwart.* Leipzig 1925.

Peligot, Eugène-M., *Douze leçons sur l'art de la verrerie.* Paris 1862.

Peligot, Eugène-M., *Le Verre, son histoire, sa fabrication.* Paris 1877.

Polak, Ada, *Modern Glass.* London 1962.

Prouvé, Madeleine, *Victor Prouvé*, Nancy, 1958.

Les Rénovateurs de l'art appliqué de 1890 à 1910—Catalogue de l'Exposition au Musée Galliéra. Paris 1925.

Revi, Albert Christian, *Nineteenth Century Glass.* London 1977.

La Revue de l'Art ancien et moderne. Paris 1902.

Rheims, Maurice, *L'Art 1900, ou le style Jules Verne.* Paris 1965.

Rosenthal, Léon, *La Verrerie française depuis cinquante ans.* Paris and Bruxelles 1927.

Sauzay, Alexandre, *Musée de la Renaissance. Série F. Notice de la verrerie et des vitraux.* Paris 1867.

Sauzay, Alexandre, *La Verrerie depuis les temps les plus reculés jusqu'à nos jours.* Paris 1884.

Sizeranne, Robert de la, *Ruskin et la religion de la beauté.* Paris 1897. *Les Sources du XXe siècle—Catalogue de l'Exposition du Musée d'Art moderne.* Paris 1960.

Sterner, Gabriele, *Daum* (doctoral thesis).

Théophile, le moine, *Schuola Diversarium Artium*, trans. by Charles de l'Escalopier. Paris 1843.

Tschudi Madsen, Stephan, *L'Art Nouveau*, trans. by L. Hinsch. Paris 1967.

Varenne, Gaston, "L'Art et la pensée d'Emile Gallé," *Mercure de France*, July 1910.

Vidalenc, Georges, *La Transformation des Arts décoratifs au XIXe siècle: William Morris son oeuvre et son influence* (doctoral thesis). Caen 1914.

Vose, Ruth Hurst, *Glass.* London 1975.

Walberg, Patrick, "Modern Style," *L'Oeil*, No. 71, Nov. 1960. Lausanne.

Webber, Norman W., *Collecting Glass.* New York 1973.

Weiss, Gustave, *The Book of Glass.* New York 1971.

Weyl, Woldemar A., *Coloured Glasses.* Sheffield 1951.

Wolf, J., *Le Travail et le façonnage décoratif du verre.* Paris 1932.

INDEX

PHOTOGRAPHIC CREDITS

Cahiers de la céramique et des arts du feu: 268-272, 282, p. 168. Connaissance des arts, Paris: 91; J. Guillot, Paris: 48, 76, 137; Mangin Photo, Nancy: 82, 132, 212, 233; Pierre Noël, Charleroi: 16, 97, 168, 192; Service de documentation photographique de la Réunion des Musées Nationaux, Paris: 101-103, 105, 107-108, 206, 295-296; Studio de Septenville, Montrouge: 2, 4-8, 10-13, 18-27, 29-32, 34, 39-52, 54, 56, 58-70, 72-100, 102, 106, 109-110, 112-120, 122-162, 164, 166-191, 193-205, 207-209, 212-218, 220-237, 239-242, 244-250, 254-259, 261-266, 273-274, 276-278, 280-281, 283, 289-291, 293.